ECONOMIC INTERDEPENDENCE IN THE ASIA-PACIFIC REGION

In 1985 the Plaza Accord initiated a global realignment of exchange rates. This has resulted in phenomenal economic growth and integration in the Asia-Pacific region and, in contrast, the decline of US economic hegemony. Based on these emerging trends, C.H. Kwan explores the possibility of self-sustaining growth in the Asia-Pacific area and the formation of a yen bloc.

Economic Interdependence in the Asia-Pacific Region: Towards a Yen Bloc brings an analytical approach to recent macroeconomic developments in this area and focuses on the 'real' and 'monetary' aspects of creating a yen bloc. The author discusses the 'real' factors of intra-regional trade and direct foreign investment. This involves a study of how Japan has replaced the USA as Asia's most important source of FDI, while the Asian NIEs have themselves emerged as major investors in the region. As the area becomes more economically integrated, national borders have become less of a barrier to economic activity. This integration has also been extended to include the socialist states. 'Monetary' factors are examined in the context of exchange-rate fluctuations, balance of payments, and ultimately, the 'internationalization of the yen' or the use of the yen as the key currency in the Asia-Pacific region. The analysis is drawn across a range of countries so that chapters are organized around issues rather than individual states. The arguments are amply supported by charts and tables. Highly technical details are contained in separate appendices so as not to upset the flow of the discussion. The author exploits his wide experience in both Asia and Japan to present a balanced view of this controversial subject.

C.H. Kwan is Senior Economist and Head of Asian Research at the Nomura Research Institute. He has extensive research experience in both Japan and the Asia-Pacific region.

ECONOMIC INTERDEPENDENCE IN THE ASIA-PACIFIC REGION

Towards a yen bloc

C.H. Kwan

London and New York

First published 1994
by Routledge
11 New Fetter Lane, London EC4P 4EE

Simultaneously published in the USA and Canada
by Routledge
29 West 35th Street, New York, NY 10001

Reprinted 1995

Typeset in Scantext September by
Solidus (Bristol) Limited
Printed in Great Britain by
Antony Rowe Ltd., Chippenham, Wiltshire

British Library Cataloguing in Publication Data
A catalogue record for this book is available from the British Library.

ISBN 0-415-10176-X

Library of Congress Cataloguing-in-Publication Data
A catalogue record for this book is available from the Library of Congress.

ISBN 0-415-10176-X

To Yuko and Megumi

CONTENTS

FIGURES

LIST OF FIGURES

TABLES

PREFACE AND
ACKNOWLEDGEMENTS

This book integrates my research carried out at the Nomura Research Institute over the last six years on macroeconomic issues in the Asia-Pacific region. During the period under study, the Asian economies have undergone dynamic changes in their economic structures and patterns of economic growth, prompted by the global realignment of exchange rates since the 1985 Plaza Accord. Interdependence among themselves has been deepening on the back of rising intra-regional trade and investment, while their dependence on the United States has fallen sharply.

Based on these emerging trends, this book explores the possibility of forming a yen bloc in the Asia-Pacific region. It tries to distinguish itself from other books on this subject in the following ways. First, in addition to the 'real' aspect of interdependence based on trade and investment, the 'monetary' aspect of a yen bloc based on the use of the yen as a key currency is emphasized. Second, by taking advantage of the author's experience in both Asia and Japan, the book aims at a more balanced view on this very controversial subject. Third, it offers a regional perspective and interdependence among Asian nations is emphasized. Fourth, it analyses more than it describes, focusing on the causes and implications of the emerging trends in the Asian economies. Fifth, it uses the tools of both macroeconomics and development economics. Short-term and long-term issues are linked by analysing the relations between economic structure and the pattern of short-term economic fluctuations. No books written by academics meet all five criteria, while books written by journalists usually meet none of them.

In the course of preparing this book, I have benefited from the excellent research facilities at the Nomura Research Institute. The unique approach at NRI, combining business and academic research, has broadened my outlook and has helped me strike a better balance between rigour and relevance. On the input side, I have benefited from NRI's global information network, and from participation in the Tokyo Club* project which has given me the chance to exchange opinions with scholars from leading think-tanks around the world. On the output side, the need to serve institutional investors, who are always demanding, has kept me abreast of the latest economic trends and informed me of new issues of interest.

Most of the papers that form the basis of this book were first published by the Tokyo Club Foundation for Global Studies. Although some of them have attracted wide coverage in the press, the full text of each paper has had only limited circulation. In the present form, I hope they become more accessible to researchers, policymakers, financial analysts, and students who are interested in the dynamism of the Asia-Pacific region.

This book would not have been possible without the support and encouragement of my colleagues at NRI, to whom I owe a great debt. Hirohiko Okumura, research director, shaped my direction of research by suggesting that I focus on the triangular economic relations among the Asian countries, the United States and Japan. Kiyohiko Fukushima, director of the Policy Research Center, introduced me to Tokyo Club activities and also initiated the idea of publishing my papers in book form. Masanobu Otsuka, general manager of the Policy Research Center, whose comments are always critical but enlightening, spared time for fruitful discussions. I am also grateful to Yuichi Kitamura, Arami Kurai, Atsushi Sumani, Howard Smith, Makiko Smith, Fumiko Sasaki, Teruko Hippo, Eri Muroga and Kayoko Senda, who all provided me with excellent research assistance at various stages. Last but not least, I would like to thank Jim Rollo of the Royal Institute of International Affairs (a member of the Tokyo Club network of global think-tanks) who did me a big favour by introducing me to the book's publisher.

C.H. Kwan

*The Tokyo Club Foundation for Global Studies was founded by the Nomura Securities Co. in 1987. The aim of the foundation is to gather wisdom from the world's leading research organizations and scholars to produce creative proposals for solving global economic problems.

EXPLANATORY NOTE

Geographic coverage

Our focus will be on the developing countries in the Asia-Pacific Region – the Asian NIEs, the ASEAN countries, and China. Unless otherwise stated, the Asian NIEs refer to South Korea, Taiwan, Hong Kong and Singapore. They are also known as the Asian NICs, but for the sake of consistency, the former is used throughout in this book. The ASEAN (Association of Southeast Asian Nations) countries refer to Indonesia, Malaysia, the Philippines and Thailand. Singapore, a full member of ASEAN will be excluded when we refer to the ASEAN countries to avoid double counting, while Brunei, the sixth member of ASEAN, will not be considered because of the lack of economic statistics. Greater China refers to China, Taiwan and Hong Kong. The Asia-Pacific region, includes the Asian NIEs, ASEAN, China and Japan.

ABBREVIATIONS

AFTA	ASEAN Free Trade Area
ANZCERTA	Australia-New Zealand Closer Economic Relationship Trade Agreement
APEC	Asia-Pacific Economic Cooperation
ASEAN	Association of Southeast Asian Nations
BIS	Bank of International Settlements
D.W.	Durbin-Watson statistics
EAEC	East Asia Economic Caucus
EC	European Community
EER	Effective Exchange Rate
FDI	Foreign Direct Investment
GATT	General Agreement on Tariffs and Trade
GDP	Gross Domestic Product
GNP	Gross National Product
GSP	Generalized System of Preferences
IMF	International Monetary Fund
JETRO	Japan External Trade Organisation
MoF	Ministry of Finance
MFN	Most Favoured Nation
NAFTA	North American Free Trade Agreement
NIEs (NICs)	Newly Industrializing Economies (Countries)
NRI	Nomura Research Institute
ODA	Official Development Aid
OECD	Organization for Economic Cooperation and Development
OPEC	Organization of Petroleum Exporting Countries
PPP	Purchasing Power Parities
REER	Real Effective Exchange Rate
SDR	Special Drawing Rights

SITC	(United Nations) Standard International Trade Classification
USTR	United States Trade Representative
bil	billion (1,000 million)
mil	million
m-o-m	month-on-month rate of change
y-o-y	year-on-year rate of change
$	US dollar (unless otherwise stated, dollar refers to US dollar).
¥	yen

1

AN OVERVIEW

THE MAIN THEMES

The Asian economies have undergone dynamic changes in their economic structure and pattern of economic growth since the 1985 Plaza Accord. Interdependence among themselves has deepened thanks to rising intra-regional trade and investment, while their dependence on the United States has fallen sharply. Against this background, the economic growth rates of the Asian countries no longer follow the growth rate of the United States. Instead, exchange-rate fluctuations and the resulting changes in the flows of trade and foreign direct investment have become the major determinants of short-term economic growth. At the same time, the integration of the socialist countries into the regional economy has been gathering momentum. The Asian countries have become more and more integrated economically and national borders have become less and less a barrier to economic activities. Based on these emerging trends, this book explores the possibility of self-sustaining growth and the formation of a yen bloc in the Asia-Pacific region.

The transition to self-sustaining growth

Despite a prolonged recession in the world economy since 1990, the Asian economies have maintained steady growth (Figure 1.1). The Asian NIEs and the ASEAN countries as a group grew 5.3 per cent in 1992, while China achieved double-digit growth. This reflects not only Asian countries' higher potential growth rates compared with the world average, but also the growing ability of these countries to generate demand from within the region.

The weakening link between economic growth in Asia and economic

1

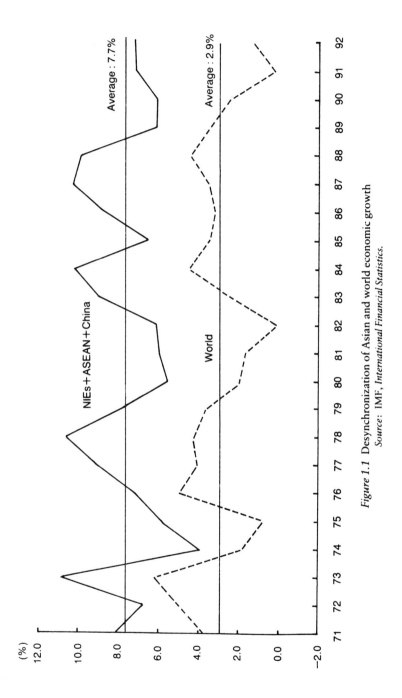

Figure 1.1 Desynchronization of Asian and world economic growth
Source: IMF, *International Financial Statistics.*

growth in the world can be confirmed by estimating the elasticity of the economic growth rate of the former with respect to changes in the latter. As shown in Figure 1.2, a 1.0 per cent increase (decrease) in the economic growth rate of the world tended to raise (reduce) that of Asia (NIEs and ASEAN) by 1.5 per cent in the 1970s. The figure has fallen to only 0.4 per cent in the last ten years. This largely reflects the desynchronization between Asian and US economic growth rates. A 1.0 per cent increase in the US economic growth rate now tends only to raise Asian economic growth by 0.3 per cent, compared with 1.0 per cent back in the 1970s. The Asian countries are thus less vulnerable than before to a recession in the global or the US economy. The other side of the same coin, however, is that the positive effect on Asian economic growth of a recovery in the world (or US) economy will be limited.

Despite these dramatic changes, the (mis)perception that Asia's economic performance is still basically determined by that of the industrial countries has persisted. Most economists still focus on the US

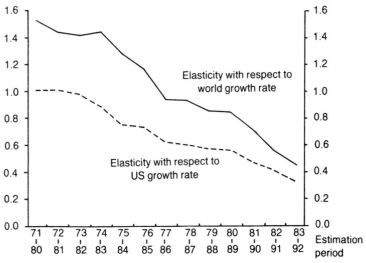

Figure 1.2 Weakening link between Asian and world growth rates

Note: The average growth rate of the Asian NIEs and ASEAN (ASIA) is estimated using the world economic growth rate (world) in the form ASIA = $a + b$(world), for the periods 1971–80, 1972–81, …, 1983–92. The parameter b measures the elasticity of Asian economic growth with respect to world economic growth, while the constant term a shows the level of Asian economic growth determined independently of the world economic growth rate. The process is then repeated using the US economic growth rate instead of the world economic growth rate as the explanatory variable. The above figure shows the changes over time of the values of b corresponding to different estimation periods.

Source: NRI.

economic growth rate when projecting economic growth in the Asian countries, while they should in fact be paying more attention to regional and domestic factors.

Factors favouring self-sustaining growth in Asia include rising intra-regional trade and foreign direct investment, and the integration of the socialist countries, notably China, into the regional economy.

Deepening intra-regional interdependence reflects the surge in intra-regional trade and investment since 1985. The relative decline in US economic power and rising trade friction between nations on either side of the Pacific have prompted Asian countries to diversify their export markets and to trade more among themselves. At the same time, Japan has replaced the United States as Asia's most important source of foreign direct investment, while the Asian NIEs have also emerged as major investors in the region. The increase in foreign direct investment among the Asian countries has boosted intra-regional trade.

The shift of Asian exports from the United States to countries in the Asia-Pacific region has accelerated (Figure 1.3). A look at exports of the Asian countries (including Japan) broken down by region shows that the share of intra-regional trade rose from 30.9 per cent of total exports in 1986 to 43.1 per cent in 1992. In contrast, the share of exports to the US market fell from 34.1 per cent to 24.2 per cent over the same period. (At the same time, Asia has replaced the United States as Japan's largest market.) On the other hand, the share of Asia (including Japan) of total

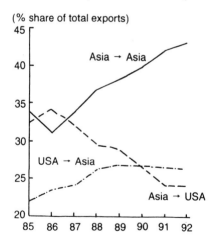

Figure 1.3 Growing importance of intra-regional trade
Note: Asia includes Japan.
Source: Compiled by NRI based on IMF, *Direction of Trade*.

US exports has risen in recent years to exceed the US share of total Asian exports.

At the same time, the inflow of foreign direct investment has become a major factor determining economic growth in the Asian countries. In the ASEAN countries, in particular, their average economic growth rate has followed closely the trends in the inflow of foreign direct investment from Japan (Figure 1.4).

With the Asia-Pacific region expected to grow at twice the US rate (three time the US rate when Japan is excluded) in the rest of the 1990s, the share of intra-regional trade will continue to increase and that of exports to the United States will continue to decline. On the other hand, the Asia-Pacific region will grow in importance as a market for US exports. Reflecting the changing pattern of trade and investment, the traditional economic relations in the Pacific region characterized by unilateral dependence of Asian countries on the United States is giving way to relations characterized by Pan-Pacific interdependence.

In addition to deepening intra-regional interdependence among the traditional high-growth economies, the expansion of their new frontiers has helped sustain economic growth in the Asia-Pacific region. This trend has been promoted by the end of the Cold War, economic reform and the open-door policy of the socialist countries in the region on one hand, and growing complementarity in the economic structures of

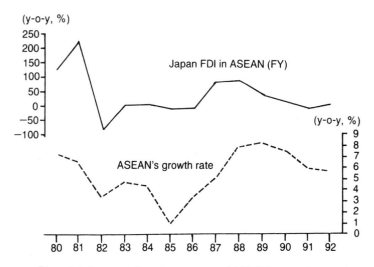

Figure 1.4 Japanese direct investment and ASEAN economic growth
Source: Japanese MoF for FDI.

countries on both sides of the new frontier on the other. Countries on the more advanced side of the frontier provide funds, technology, management know-how and infrastructure, while countries on the less developed side provide labour, land and natural resources. At the same time, recent progress in multilateral cooperation among Asian countries at the government-to-government level will accelerate economic integration among countries in the Asia-Pacific region.

The Asia-Pacific region's transition to self-sustaining growth, however, would not be complete without Japan expanding its imports from the Asian countries. This would require further progress in Japan's recent efforts to open its market for imports. Failure to reduce the trade imbalance between Japan and its neighbours would lead to new sources of trade friction, with adverse effect on intra-regional trade.

Formation of a yen bloc

The establishment of a yen bloc – a grouping of countries which use the yen as an international currency and maintain stable exchange rates against the yen – has attracted growing interest in recent years against a background of growing Japanese economic and financial power, deepening economic interdependence between Japan and its Asian neighbours, and monetary integration in the EC. The traditional approach to this issue, couched in terms of 'the internationalization of the yen', has a distinctively Japanese perspective. What is also needed, however, is a perspective of the advantages and disadvantages to the Asian countries that are supposed to be potential members of the bloc.

The yen–dollar rate has become a major determinant of short-term economic growth in the Asian countries. Indeed, economic growth rates in the Asian NIEs now follows more closely trends in the yen–dollar rate than the US economic growth rate, which is usually considered to have the dominant effect on these economies (Figure 1.5).

The effect of yen–dollar rate fluctuations on the Asian economies differs from country to country, depending on the differences in their trade structures and the resulting differences in their trade relations with Japan. For the Asian NIEs, which compete with Japan in international markets, economic growth rates tend to rise as the yen appreciates and to decline as the yen depreciates. An appreciation of the yen raises their export prices (or output prices) more than their import prices (or input prices). The resulting improvement in their terms of trade (or profits) in turn boosts output. By contrast, a depreciation of the yen reduces export prices more than import prices and the resulting fall in profits in turn

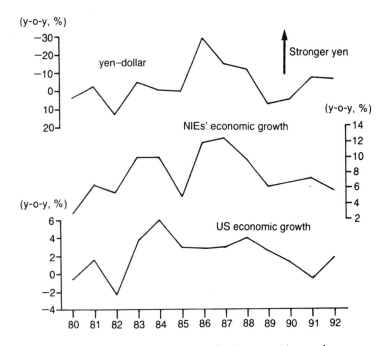

Figure 1.5 The yen–dollar rate and NIEs' economic growth
Source: Compiled by NRI based on IMF, *International Financial Statistics.*

reduces output. The reverse may be true for the ASEAN countries, which do not compete much with Japan, but depend heavily on it for imports. An appreciation of the yen, for example, raises their import prices more than their export prices, and the resulting squeeze on profits reduces output.

For the Asian countries, output fluctuations associated with changes in the yen–dollar rate can be stabilized by manipulating the exchange rate of the domestic currency against the dollar. For the Asian NIEs, the increase in output associated with an appreciation of the yen can be offset by revaluing the local currency, which suppresses output by squeezing profits. In contrast, for the ASEAN countries, stabilization of output requires devaluing the domestic currency when the yen appreciates and revaluing it when the yen depreciates.

Output stabilization can also be achieved by pegging to a basket of currencies. In general, to stabilize output, a country should peg its currency to a basket with large weights for competitors' currencies and small or even negative weights for major suppliers' currencies. It follows therefore that the Asian NIEs may benefit by pegging their currencies to the yen, though the ASEAN economies may be destabilized by a yen-peg. Other things being equal, the Asian NIEs have more incentive than the ASEAN countries to peg their exchange rates to the yen.

The volatility of the Asian currencies against the yen seems to be a major factor restraining the use of the yen as an international currency in Asia. If the Asian countries shift their current exchange rate regimes from pegging loosely to the dollar to pegging to the yen (or to a basket of currencies in which the yen carries substantial weight), more Asian importers and exporters would prefer invoicing in yen instead of dollars; and borrowers and investors would be willing to hold a larger portion of their portfolios in yen-denominated financial assets.

By lowering the risk associated with exchange-rate fluctuations, pegging to the yen may benefit Asian countries by expanding their trade with Japan as well as their capital inflows from Japan. This has become all the more important now that Japan has replaced the United States as the largest investor in Asia, and that the United States alone can no longer play the role of locomotive for the Asian economies.

THE COMMON PREMISES

Characteristic of the Asia-Pacific region

The Asia-Pacific economy can be characterized by dynamism in economic growth, diversity in the level of economic development and economic structure, and heavy dependence on international trade and investment.

The Asia-Pacific region has been the most dynamic part of the world economy throughout the post-war period. Through trade and investment, the wave of industrialization that spread from Japan to the Asian NIEs in the 1960s is now spreading to ASEAN and China. Economic growth in the Asian NIEs averaged over 8 per cent a year in the last three decades despite two oil crises in the 1970s, a sluggish world economy in the first half of the 1980s, and rising protectionism and currency appreciation in the latter half of the 1980s. Economic growth in the ASEAN countries, which had lagged far behind the Asian NIEs until the mid-1980s, picked up in the last few years thanks to the rapid increase in foreign direct investment. Economic growth in China has accelerated since the late 1970s when the government shifted to an open-door policy that promotes foreign investment and exports.

Rapid economic development in the Asian countries has been accompanied by a rapid transformation of economic structures. The most drastic changes have occurred in their commodity compositions of exports; the share of manufactured goods has risen rapidly at the expense of primary commodities. Indeed, all four Asian NIEs now ranks among the world's top twenty exporters of manufactured goods.

The Asian countries have very open economies, reflecting their development strategy of relying on the inflow of foreign capital on the supply side and on exports on the demand side. This contrasts with the import-substitution strategy pursued by most Latin American countries. Merchandise exports as a percentage of GNP, for example, are much higher than other parts of the world (Figure 1.6). As a result, economic performance in these countries is highly vulnerable to developments beyond their national borders. In the past, the world (or US) economic growth rate had the largest effect on Asian economic growth. Recent changes in the pattern of trade and investment, however, has shifted the major determinants of economic performance in the Asian countries to more regional factors. It is interesting to note that the declining trend in the Asian NIEs' dependence on exports contrasts sharply with the rising trend in ASEAN and China.

The Asia-Pacific region consists of countries with levels of economic development ranging over a very wide spectrum. Japan, with a GNP of $3,700 billion and a per capita GNP of $29,800 in 1992, is a global power. Hong Kong and Singapore, the two city-states and trading and financial centres of the region have per capita income on a par with that of Australia. At the other end of the spectrum, China, Indonesia and the Philippines only have per capita GNP of less than $1,000, a level considered relatively low even by the standards of the developing countries.

The differences in economic structures, which to a large extent reflect the differences in the level of economic development, have strong implications for the pattern of growth and interdependence in the Asia-Pacific region. A stronger yen, for example, may boost economic growth in the Asian NIEs which compete with Japan in export markets and harm other Asian countries which depend heavily on Japan for imports. Likewise, an increase in oil prices may benefit Malaysia and Indonesia, the two major oil exporters in the region, but hurts other net importers of oil. At the same time, rapid transformation in economic structures in the course of economic development has led to drastic changes in the pattern of interdependence over time.

Reflecting the openness and diversity of the region, dynamic changes in the Asian economy can be characterized by the 'flying-geese pattern'

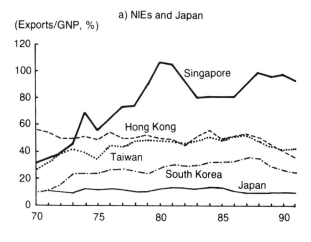

a) NIEs and Japan

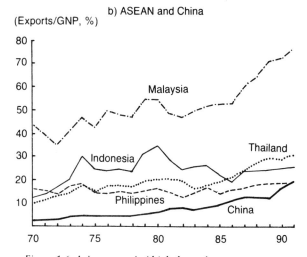

b) ASEAN and China

Figure 1.6 Asian countries' high dependence on exports
Note: Figures for Hong Kong and Singapore exclude re-exports.
Source: Compiled by NRI based on IMF, *International Financial Statistics* and official
statistics of Hong Kong and Taiwan.

(Akamatsu, 1962), in which economic changes in the more advanced
countries are repeated with time lags in the less developed ones. Foreign
direct investment from the former to the latter usually plays a dominant
role in the transmission of these changes. The flying-geese model has
found applications in a wide range of issues relating to the interdependence among Asian countries. For example, it has been widely

10

used to describe the spreading of industrialization from Japan to the Asian NIEs and then further to the ASEAN countries and China.[1] In Chapter 2 we apply it to examine the evolution of trade imbalances between the two sides of the Pacific in the second half of the 1980s. In Chapter 5 the flying-geese pattern provides a framework to study the Asian countries' commodity compositions of trade in the course of catching-up with the advanced countries.

The changing balance of power in the global economy

The drastic changes in the pattern of trade and interdependence in Asia reflects to a large extent the shifting balance of power in the world economy – a trend which has accelerated since the September 1985 Plaza Accord. The 1980s witnessed the continued decline of US economic hegemony and the emergence of Japan, and to a lesser extent, the Asian NIEs and China, as major players in the world economy.

Robust economic growth in the Asian economies has led to a rapid expansion of their size. In the last thirty years, real GNP multiplied 12 times in the Asian NIEs, 11 times in Japan and 6 times in ASEAN and China. This compares with 2.5 times for the United States and 3 times for the world economy. Rapid economic growth in the Asian developing countries expanded the size of their economies and reduced the gap that separates them from advanced countries. The change in the balance of power in the world economy is apparent when we look at the regional composition of world trade (Table 1.1).

The Asia-Pacific region has emerged as one of the world's top trading regions, with its share of world trade increasing from 14.6 per cent in 1980 to 22.3 per cent in 1992. The growing importance of the region parallels the growing economic clout of Japan and the Asian NIEs, which together account for three-quarters of the region's total trade. The Asian NIEs' share of world trade reached 9.3 per cent in 1992 and their share of world imports has surpassed that of Japan since 1987. The four Asian NIEs now rank among the world's top twenty trading countries. They also house five of the world's top ten container ports.[2]

China and the ASEAN countries are also catching up from behind. China's share of world trade has doubled since the late 1970s, when the government shifted to an open-door economic policy. In the second half of the 1980s, trade in the ASEAN countries recovered from a trough on the back of the recovery in the prices of primary commodities and rising foreign direct investment in the manufacturing sector.

In contrast, the US share of world trade fell in the second half of the

11

Table 1.1 Regional breakdown of world trade

Country/Region	World share %								
	1980	1985	1986	1987	1988	1989	1990	1991	1992
Exports United States	11.6	11.8	11.0	10.6	11.9	12.5	11.8	12.3	12.3
Japan	6.9	9.8	10.6	9.8	9.8	9.4	8.6	9.2	9.3
Asian NIEs	4.0	6.3	6.7	7.6	8.3	8.5	8.0	8.9	9.4
ASEAN	2.5	2.5	2.1	2.2	2.4	2.6	2.6	2.9	3.1
China	1.0	1.5	1.6	1.7	1.8	1.8	1.8	2.0	2.2
Asia-Pacific(a)	14.4	20.1	21.0	21.3	22.3	22.3	21.1	23.0	24.0
EC(b)	36.5	35.9	40.3	40.7	39.6	38.9	41.2	39.9	39.8
N. America(c)	15.2	16.8	14.4	14.8	16.3	16.6	15.7	16.0	16.0
(a)+(b)+(c)	66.1	72.8	75.7	76.8	78.2	77.8	77.9	78.9	79.8
Imports United States	13.2	19.1	18.8	17.4	16.7	16.4	15.1	14.3	14.7
Japan	7.3	6.9	6.2	6.2	6.8	7.0	6.9	6.7	6.2
Asian NIEs	4.5	5.7	5.7	6.4	7.6	7.9	7.8	8.7	9.3
ASEAN	2.0	2.0	1.7	1.8	2.1	2.5	2.8	3.2	3.3
China	1.0	2.2	2.1	1.8	2.0	1.9	1.6	1.8	2.0
Asia-Pacific(a)	14.8	16.8	15.7	16.2	18.5	19.3	19.1	20.3	20.8
EC(b)	39.7	35.1	37.9	39.2	39.1	38.8	41.3	40.9	40.3
N. America(c)	16.3	23.3	21.5	21.1	20.7	20.4	18.6	17.8	18.1
(a)+(b)+(c)	70.8	75.2	75.1	76.5	78.3	78.5	79.0	79.1	79.2
Total Trade United States	12.4	15.5	15.0	14.1	14.3	14.5	13.5	13.3	13.5
Japan	7.1	8.3	8.4	8.0	8.3	8.2	7.7	7.9	7.7
Asian NIEs	4.3	6.0	6.2	7.0	7.9	8.2	7.9	8.8	9.3
ASEAN	2.2	2.2	1.9	2.0	2.2	2.5	2.7	3.1	3.2
China	1.0	1.9	1.8	1.7	1.9	1.9	1.7	1.9	2.1
Asia-Pacific(a)	14.6	18.4	18.3	18.7	20.3	20.8	20.1	21.7	22.3
EC(b)	38.1	35.5	39.0	39.9	39.4	38.9	41.2	40.4	40.0
N. America(c)	15.8	20.1	18.0	18.0	18.5	18.6	17.1	16.9	17.1
(a)+(b)+(c)	68.5	74.0	75.3	76.6	78.2	78.3	78.5	79.0	79.5

Source: IMF, *International Financial Statistics.*

1980s. In particular, its share of world imports dropped from 19.1 per cent in 1985 to 14.7 per cent in 1992, reflecting slower economic growth and the need to reduce its immense trade deficit.

The Asia-Pacific region also boasts the world's largest foreign exchange reserves (Figure 1.7). Japan, the Asian NIEs, ASEAN and China together had reserves totalling $303 billion at the end of 1991, surpassing those of the twelve members of the EC combined. Indeed, Taiwan alone has the world's largest foreign exchange reserves ($82 billion at the end of 1992).

Exchange-rate realignment since 1985

The global realignment of exchange rates in the second half of the 1980s has been the major factor determining macroeconomic performance and the changing pattern of trade and interdependence in the Asia-Pacific region.

The global exchange rate realignment in the second half of the 1980s was made necessary by the growing exchange rate mis-alignment

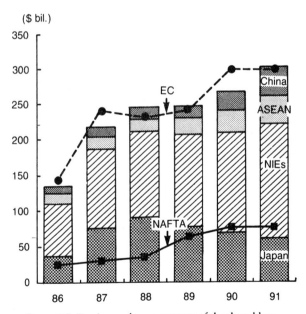

Figure 1.7 Foreign exchange reserves of the three blocs
Source: IMF, *International Financial Statistics* and official statistics of Taiwan and Hong Kong.

among the major currencies in the first half. The combination of monetary tightening and fiscal expansion in the United States under the Reagan Administration led to high interest rates and massive inflows of foreign capital, which in turn boosted the US dollar.[3] The strengthening of the US dollar in the first half of the 1980s, however, coincided with the build-up of large deficits in the US current account. By 1985, the United States had become a net debtor country and fears of a dollar crisis loomed. It was against this background that the five major industrial countries decided to orchestrate a coordinated devaluation of the US dollar when their ministers of finance and central bank governors met in the Plaza Hotel in New York in September 1985.

The strengthening of the yen, in particular, had the strongest impact on the Asian economies. The yen started to recover from its trough against the dollar in February 1985 – a trend that accelerated after the Plaza Agreement. The appreciation of the yen in the mid-1980s coincided with the emergence of Japan as the world's largest creditor country. In 1986 and 1987, when the yen was rising sharply against the dollar, the international competitiveness of Asian NIEs' exports improved substantially vis-à-vis Japan. The resulting surge in exports and inflow of foreign direct investment from Japan pushed economic growth in the Asian NIEs into double digits in 1986 and 1987. The combined current account surpluses of these countries jumped to more than $30 billion in 1987; their trade surplus with the United States alone reached $34.1 billion, or 22.4 per cent of the total US trade deficit. The offshoot of the NIEs' trading success was that they could no longer be ignored when considering global trade imbalances.

Against the backdrop of expanding trade imbalances, trade friction with the United States escalated and in 1986 the United States began to pressure the Asian NIEs to revalue their currencies. Currency appreciation, coupled with rising wages, led to a deceleration in export growth and a shift in the engine of economic growth from net exports to domestic demand – trends which became even more apparent in 1989 when the Asian NIEs were stripped of the privileges enjoyed under the US Generalized System of Preferences and when their currencies appreciated not only against the dollar but also against the yen. With the attractiveness of investing in the Asian NIEs declining, Japanese multinationals began to shift their foreign direct investment to the ASEAN countries in 1987. They were followed by manufacturers in the Asian NIEs, who had been granted more freedom to invest abroad as the national current accounts moved into surplus.

In the south, the ASEAN economies emerged from the doldrums in

1987 on the back of a rebound in commodity prices and of a surge in the foreign direct investment inflows from Japan and the Asian NIEs. The recovery coincided with a major shift from import substitution to export promotion in the ASEAN countries' development policies. The surge in foreign direct investment inflows into the manufacturing sector, by relaxing bottlenecks in the supply of funds and technology, built the foundation for an economic takeoff.

THE PLAN OF THE BOOK

With these common premises in mind, we elaborate on the main themes in the chapters that follow. Our framework of analysis is presented in Figure 1.8, which also shows the relations between individual chapters of this book.

Chapter 2 studies Asian countries' balance of payments. The emergence of the Asian NIEs as creditor countries is examined using the framework of the 'balance-of-payments cycle'. In addition, the interaction between the balance of payments and the exchange-rate realignment in the Asia-Pacific region in the latter half of the 1980s is analysed.

Chapter 3 reviews Asian countries' macroeconomic performance since the mid-1980s. Fluctuations in exchange rates, particularly the yen–dollar rate, are identified as the major factor determining swings in economic activity in the Asian countries.

Chapter 4 derives an optimal peg for an Asian currency when the policy objective is to minimize fluctuations in output resulting from changes in the exchange rates of third currencies, such as the yen–dollar rate. The importance of trade structure in determining the optimal peg is emphasized.

Chapter 5 describes the evolution of the Asian countries' commodity composition of trade in the course of economic development using the 'flying-geese' model. The recent trend of rising intra-industry trade, made possible by the progress in industrialization in the developing countries of the region, is also described.

Chapter 6 studies the changing regional composition of trade. Special attention is paid to trade relations between the Asian NIEs, Japan and the United States in the context of the Pacific trade triangle, and to the implications of recent changes in the commodity and regional compositions of trade for the pattern of macroeconomic interdependence.

Chapter 7 shifts the focus from the deepening of regional inter-

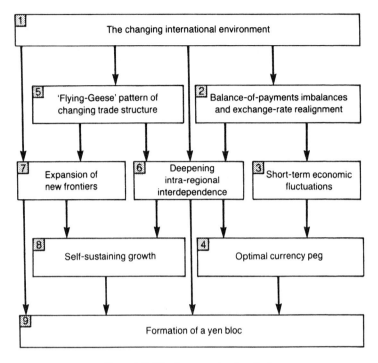

Figure 1.8 The framework of analysis
Note: Figures denote corresponding chapter numbers in this book.
Source: NRI.

dependence among the traditional high-growth economies to the expansion of their new frontiers with the socialist countries in the region. The emergence of regional economic zones is also discussed.

Chapter 8 presents our medium-term outlook for the Asian economies. In addition to the international factors emphasized in earlier chapters, domestic factors that have become more and more important in determining the medium-term economic prospects of the Asian countries are taken into consideration.

The concluding chapter studies the formation of a yen bloc in the Asia-Pacific region based on our analysis of the emerging pattern of trade and interdependence. By focusing on the implications for output stability in the Asian countries if they peg their currencies to the yen, the chapter offers an Asian perspective of the issue, which has so far been missing in the literature.

A yen bloc has both a 'real' aspect based on intra-regional trade and investment and a 'monetary' aspect based on the use of the yen as a key currency in the Asia-Pacific region. In Chapters 5 to 8 we focus on the real aspect, and in Chapters 2 to 4 and Chapter 9 we emphasize the monetary aspect.

2

BALANCE-OF-PAYMENTS
IMBALANCES AND
EXCHANGE-RATE
REALIGNMENT

INTRODUCTION

The availability of foreign capital is a major determinant of macro-economic performance in developing countries. During the 1970s, the abundant supply of savings amongst the OPEC Arab states allowed developing countries to borrow at low interest rates and achieve high economic growth. The situation reversed in the 1980s. With oil prices weakening, the current account of the OPEC countries turned into a deficit in the early 1980s. Coupled with the rise in global interest rates resulting from the widening fiscal deficit in the United States, the debt situation in the developing countries deteriorated and the flow of funds into these countries stopped. Indeed, there was a substantial diversion of funds from the developing countries to the United States. Developing countries in general, and the heavily indebted Latin American countries in particular, were forced to take austerity measures to curb imports, with adverse effects on economic growth.

In contrast to Latin American countries, Asian countries (except the Philippines) have been very successful in utilizing foreign capital in promoting economic development without incurring serious debt problems. This largely reflects their development strategy of export promotion and reliance on foreign direct investment over borrowing as a means to finance the current account deficit. The Asian NIEs as a group have already attained creditor country status; the large current account surpluses recorded in the 1980s have allowed them to repay their debt and accumulate foreign assets. The improvement in their current account balances also put upward pressure on their currencies in the latter half of the 1980s. On the other hand, the ASEAN countries are still relying on foreign capital to bridge the gap between investment need and domestic savings.

This chapter studies the balance of payments of the Asian countries. After examining the long-term trends in the Asian countries' balance of payments, it focuses on the interaction between trade imbalances and exchange rates in the Asia-Pacific region in the latter half of the 1980s.

LONG-TERM TRENDS IN THE BALANCE OF PAYMENTS

The balance-of-payments cycle[1]

The balance-of-payments cycle provides a framework for studying the long-term trend in the balance of payments. A country's balance-of-payments position can be classified into six categories – young debtor, mature debtor, debt reducer, young creditor, mature creditor, and asset liquidator – according to the combinations of plus and minus signs on the balances of the trade (goods and services) account, on the investment income account, and on the current account.[2] Because a country usually passes from one category to the next in a regular sequence, this can be referred to as the six stages of the balance-of-payments cycle (Table 2.1).[3]

A country in the young debtor stage relies heavily on funds borrowed from abroad to finance its investment projects. The current account, the investment income account and the trade account are in the red, reflecting heavy interest payments as well as low export capacity and the need to import foreign capital goods.

Table 2.1 Six stages of the balance-of-payments cycle (1992)

Stage	Goods and services	Current account	Investment income	Examples (1992)
1 Young debtor	−	−	−	Thailand, Malaysia, Philippines
2 Mature debtor	+	−	−	Indonesia
3 Debt reducer	+	+	−	China
4 Young creditor	+	+	+	Japan, Taiwan
5 Mature creditor	−	+	+	Singapore, Switzerland
6 Asset liquidator	−	−	+	UK, USA

Note: Goods and services include transfer payments.
Source: NRI.

A country becomes a mature debtor when export expansion pushes the trade balance into surplus. The current account remains negative, however, as the trade surplus is not enough to offset the deficit in investment income.

A country moves to the debt reducer stage when further expansion of exports pushes its current account into surplus, allowing the country to reduce its foreign debt. The transition occurs when the surplus on the balance of goods and services becomes larger than the deficit on the balance of the investment account.

A country enters a young creditor stage when its balance of investment income also turns from a deficit into a surplus. At the same time, the country usually becomes a (net) creditor in the sense that its holding of foreign assets surpasses foreign liabilities.

A young creditor becomes a mature creditor when its trade balance turns negative again as a result of rising imports. The current account balance, however, remains positive, reflecting a large surplus in the balance of investment income. The increase in foreign assets continues to outpace that of foreign liabilities.

Finally, a country enters the asset liquidator stage when the trade deficit has become so large that the current account turns into a deficit. This implies a reduction of net foreign assets and a falling surplus in the investment account. A continuation of this trend may actually lead to a deficit in the investment income account, bringing the country back to the young debtor stage, the first stage in the balance-of-payments cycle.

The trend in the current account over the balance-of-payments can be viewed from the perspective of the investment-savings balance.[4] By the national income identity,

$$Y = C + I + (X - M)$$

where Y = National Income

C = Consumption
I = Investment
X = Exports
M = Imports

Noting that

$$S = Y - C$$

and

$$X - M = B$$

where S = Savings

B = Current account balance

we have

B = S − I

The current account balance can therefore be interpreted as the gap between savings and investment. At the early stage of development, investment far exceed domestic savings and the gap is financed mainly by borrowings from abroad. An improvement in the current account corresponds to the elimination of the excess of investment over domestic savings. In the case of Korea, for example, this has been achieved by an increase in the domestic savings rate over the last twenty years (Figure 2.1). The subsequent decline in the current account surplus reflects a sharper decline in the savings rate than in the investment rate.

The Asian countries are at different stages of the debt cycle, broadly

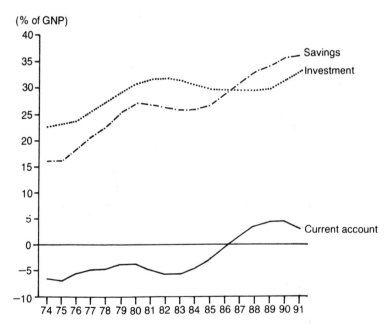

Figure 2.1 Current account and the I–S balance: the Korean case
Note: 5-year moving average.
Source: Compiled by NRI based on IMF, *International Financial Statistics*.

in line with their level of economic development. Singapore, with surpluses in its current and investment income account but a deficit in its trade account, has a balance-of-payments structure typical of a mature creditor. Taiwan, which has positive balances in all three accounts is now a young creditor. Korea which has run deficits in all three accounts recently, has slipped back to the stage of young debtor from that of debt reducer back in 1989. Korea's net foreign debt (and thus interest payments), however, has shrunk sharply from its peak level in the mid-1980s thanks to the large current account surplus recorded in 1987–9; it may not take long for Korea to achieve creditor status. The Asian NIEs as a group (excluding Hong Kong for which investment income statistics are not available) have reached the young creditor stage (Figure 2.2).

On the other hand, among the ASEAN countries, Indonesia has

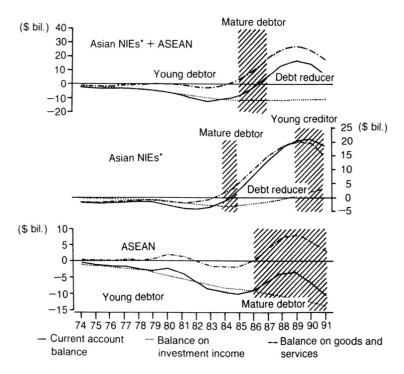

Figure 2.2 Asian countries' stages of the balance-of-payments cycle
Notes: 1 *Excluding Hong Kong. 2 Based on 5-year moving averages.
Source: Compiled by NRI based on IMF, *Balance of Payments Statistics*, and official statistics of Taiwan.

reached the mature debtor stage while the others have stayed at the young debtor stage. The ASEAN countries as a group have a balance-of-payments structure typical of a young debtor.

The current-account balances of the ASEAN countries have worsened sharply since 1988. Their combined current-account deficit jumped from $5.5 billion in 1988 to $17.5 billion in 1991. The deterioration in the current accounts, however, has not led to any financing problems in these countries, since it has largely reflected the surge in imports of capital goods accompanying the inflow of foreign direct investment which are financed automatically. Indeed, major debt indicators of these countries have improved substantially since the mid-1980s. The upward trends in the debt service ratios (total debt service on long-term debt divided by exports of goods and services) of all four countries were reversed in the latter half of the 1980s, thanks to the surge in exports. The ratios of their total debt to GNP have also dropped from their peak levels in 1987.

The ASEAN countries' current accounts should improve in the medium term. The inflow of foreign direct investment is expected to boost exports when production comes on stream, and import growth should slow down over time as the proportion of intermediate goods, parts and components that can be procured from local suppliers increases.

Taken together, the Asian NIEs (excluding Hong Kong) and the ASEAN countries reached the mature debtor stage in 1985 and the debt reducer stage in 1987. The advance of their combined current accounts from deficit to surplus implies that this region has become a net supplier of funds in international financial markets.

The improvement in the balance-of-payments position of the Asian countries in the latter half of the 1980s was at the expense of the rising US current-account deficit. The United States trade account has been in deficit since 1975 and the current account has been in deficit since 1982. With the balance in investment income remaining in the black, the United States can be classified as an asset liquidator. If the United States fails to reduce its current account deficit in the near future, it may become a young debtor again.

Japan's experience provides some hints as to the impact that an easing of current account constraints can have on economic policy.[5] Japan entered the debt reducer stage in 1964. That same year, it joined the OECD and became an IMF Article VIII country. This marked the beginning of a series of measures aimed at liberalizing foreign exchange controls. Taiwan and South Korea have begun to take similar steps.

Taiwan implemented major steps in relaxing foreign exchange controls in 1987. Following suit, South Korea changed its status to conform to IMF Article VIII in late 1988. At the same time, Korea announced plans to allow foreign investors and securities companies to participate directly in the domestic stock market in 1992. Like Japan, Taiwan and South Korea before them, other Asian countries will speed up financial liberalization when their current accounts move into the black.

A large portion of the current account surpluses of the Asian countries has accumulated in the form of foreign exchange reserves at central banks because of strict controls on private capital outflows. Indeed, the total foreign exchange reserves of Greater China – China, Taiwan and Hong Kong – totalled $165 billion at the end of 1992, almost on a par with those of Japan, Germany and the United States combined (Figure 2.3). Taiwan alone now boasts the largest foreign reserves in the world. This newly gained financial power will be used to finance some of the world's most ambitious infrastructure projects in

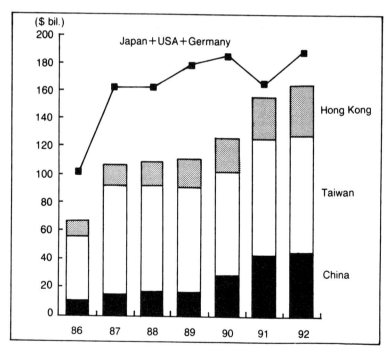

Figure 2.3 Foreign exchange reserves of Greater China
Source: IMF *International Financial Statistics* and official statistics of Hong Kong and Taiwan.

the 1990s, including Hong Kong's new airport, Taiwan's Six-Year National Development Plan and Shanghai's Pudong Development Project. At the same time, as the easing of foreign exchange controls gathers pace, direct and portfolio investment abroad by the private sector will increase substantially. Taiwan's foreign direct investment in the ASEAN countries and Fujian Province in China has in fact surged since relaxation of controls in 1987.

The global savings shortage and Asia's external balance in the 1990s[6]

The revitalization of Eastern Europe will not be possible without financial support from the West. The emergence of Eastern Europe as a competitor for funds has given rise to concern among the developing countries in Asia (particularly the ASEAN countries) that foreign capital available to them may be reduced in the medium term. This worry, however, seems to be overstated for two reasons. First, the potential demand for funds may not materialize if the current confusion accompanying the breakdown of the old system continues. Second, even if demand does appear, the reduction in military expenditures in the United States – the peace dividend – and the resulting fall in the US twin deficits should increase global savings and thus the size of the pie available to both Asia and Eastern Europe. Here we provide an optimal scenario for the global trade imbalances in the 1990s.

In terms of current account transactions, Eastern Europe will emerge as a major importer, partly offsetting the slack in global demand created by the slowdown in US imports. The Asian NIEs will find Eastern Europe an attractive market for their consumer goods while the industrial countries will increase their exports of capital goods. The diversion of the Asian NIEs' exports to Eastern Europe should help reduce their dependence on the US market and calm trade friction.

Reflecting these developments, Eastern Europe's trade deficit against Western Europe, the United States, Japan, as well as the Asian NIEs will increase (Table 2.2a). The overall US trade deficit should decline, largely as a result of an increase in its trade surplus with Eastern Europe and to a lesser extent, a reduction in its trade deficits with Japan and the Asian NIEs. On the other hand, Japan and the Asian NIEs' current accounts will continue to run substantial surpluses, with the reduction in their surpluses with the United States partly offset by an increase in their trade surpluses with Eastern Europe.

In terms of the capital account, Japan and the Asian NIEs, together with Western Europe, will remain major suppliers of funds to inter-

Table 2.2 Projected changes in the regional balance of payments in the 1990s

A \ B	USA	Japan	Asia	Europe	Total
USA		↑	↑	↑	↑
Japan	↓		→	↑	→
Asia	↓	→		↑	→
Europe	↓	↓	↓		↓

Note: Arrows denote the direction of change in country A's current account balance with country B. ↑ Improve (increase in surplus or decrease in deficit). → Unchanged.
↓ Deteriorate (decrease in surplus or increase in deficit).

A \ B	USA	Japan	Asia	Europe	Total
USA		↓	→	→	↓
Japan	↑		→	↓	→
Asia	→	→		→	→
Europe	→	↑	→		↑

Note: Arrows denote the direction of change in country A's current account balance with country B. ↑ Improve (increase in net capital inflow or decrease in net capital outflow).
→ Unchanged. ↓ Deteriorate (decrease in net capital inflow or increase in net capital outflow).
Source: NRI.

national financial markets (Table 2.2b). So far, a large part of these countries' surpluses has been used to finance the US current account deficit, but the expected decline in the US deficit in the coming years should release funds for investment in other regions. Because of historical and geographical links, Japan and the Asian NIEs will concentrate their investment in the Asia-Pacific region while Western European countries will increase their investment in Eastern Europe. Indeed, the emergence of the Asian NIEs as major investors in the ASEAN countries in the last few years has greatly reduced the relative importance of the United States and Western Europe as sources of foreign direct investment. While a diversion of official development aid (ODA) away from Asia to Eastern Europe may occur, the inflow of private capital will continue to support economic development in the Asia-Pacific region.

INTERACTION BETWEEN TRADE IMBALANCES AND EXCHANGE RATES

Trade imbalances and exchange-rate realignment[7]

With their share of world trade rivalling that of Japan and their trade surplus with the United States surging, the Asian NIEs came under mounting pressure from the industrial countries in the latter half of the 1980s to play roles in the international economy commensurate with their newly gained economic status. In the global exchange-rate realignment of 1985, which aimed at reducing global trade imbalances, the Asian NIEs were forced to appreciate their currencies along with Japan and other major European countries.

The yen started to appreciate against the dollar in February 1985 from a level of ¥260 (period average), and the pace of appreciation accelerated after the Plaza Accord in September 1985. Despite setbacks in the short run, the upward trend of the yen against the dollar continued until November 1988, when the Japanese currency hit ¥123. With economic fundamentals in the United States improving and concern over political stability in Japan growing amid the Recruit Scandal, however, the yen started to depreciate against the dollar in late 1988, a trend that lasted until mid-1990. This was followed by a rebound of the yen in the second half of 1990 against a background of monetary tightening in Japan and monetary easing in the United States.

Thanks to the sharp appreciation of the yen since 1985, the Asian NIEs' export competitiveness improved sharply and their trade surplus ballooned. By 1987, their current account surplus reached $30.6 billion, or 10.2 per cent of GNP, reflecting a surge of exports to the United States. As a result, trade friction between the two sides escalated, and the United States announced that South Korea, Taiwan, Hong Kong and Singapore would be deprived of their special tariff treatment under the Generalized System of Preferences (GSP), effective as of January 1989. At the same time, the United States stepped up pressure on these countries to revalue their currencies and open their markets to US goods and services.

In response to these demands, the Asian NIEs started to revalue their currencies in 1986. Taiwan, which has run the largest trade surplus with the United States among the Asian NIEs, allowed the New NT dollar to appreciate 54 per cent against the US dollar between early 1986 and mid-1989. Korea followed and let the won appreciate 33 per cent between mid-1986 and mid-1989. On the other hand, Hong Kong and Singapore, which have few restrictions on imports, have been subjected to much less US pressure to revalue their currencies. Indeed, the Hong Kong dollar has remained stable against the dollar since October 1983.[8] Singapore, however, has allowed its currency to appreciate at a gradual pace since 1985 to keep domestic inflation low.

The balance of payments is no doubt the most important determinant of exchange rates in the Asian NIEs. The exchange rate of the Korean won against the dollar, for example, has tracked closely developments in the country's external balance. Korea shifted from a dollar-linked exchange-rate system to a managed-float system in early 1980, which was followed by a period of steady depreciation of the won against the dollar. This trend was reversed in early 1986, and the appreciation of the won against the dollar lasted until mid-1989 (Figure 2.4). It is interesting to note that the won's rebound against the dollar in 1986 coincided with the trade balance turning from deficit to surplus, and the return of a trade deficit in 1989 prompted a reversal of the upward trend of the won rate. According to our estimates, a $1 billion increase in Korea's cumulative trade surplus tends to push up the won against the dollar by 13.6 won.

As in the case of Japan, currency appreciation in the Asian NIEs has contributed to a reduction of their external imbalances. By 1992, the combined current account surplus of the Asian NIEs had dropped to $8.1 billion, with their combined trade balance (on a customs-cleared basis) turning into a deficit (Figure 2.5). This resulted not only from a slowdown in export growth, but also from a surge in imports accompanying the firming of domestic demand and the implementation of import-liberalization measures. At the same time, to calm trade friction with the United States, South Korea made significant concessions in troubled areas such as import bans and other measures that protect local production, as well as investment barriers and import restrictions affecting agricultural products. Likewise, Taiwan promised to improve the protection of intellectual property rights. These efforts were rewarded in May 1989 when the Asian NIEs were excluded from the list of priority foreign countries under the Super 301 provision of the US Omnibus Trade Act. Since then, trade friction between the Asian

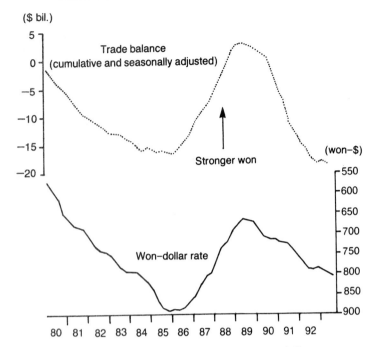

Figure 2.4 Korean balance of trade and the won–dollar rate

Notes: 1 Estimation of the won–$ rate:

won–$ = 544.5 + 4.4 (Time Trend) − 13.6 (Cumulative trade balance)
(18.23) (−28.96)
Sample period : 1980 Q1 ∼ 1990 Q4, and figures in ( ) denote t-values
R̄² = 0.953 D.W. = 0.439
2 Cumulative trade balance measured in $ bil.

Source: NRI.

NIEs and the United States has eased, and the appreciation of the NIEs' currencies (except the Singapore dollar) against the US dollar ended.

On the other hand, the ASEAN countries have been relatively free from external pressure to revalue their currencies because they are debtor countries. Indeed, their current account deficits have surged since 1988 as a result of rising imports accompanying the massive inflow of foreign direct investment. Except for the 31 per cent devaluation of the Indonesian rupiah in September 1986 and the fall of the Philippine peso in the aftermath of the Gulf Crisis, the ASEAN currencies have remained broadly stable against the US dollar.

Taken together, the exchange-rate realignment in the Asia-Pacific region since 1985 can be divided into four phases (Figure 2.6). In the

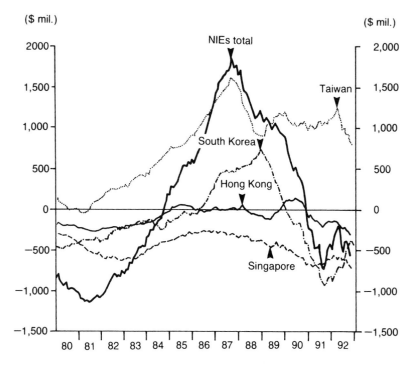

Figure 2.5 Trade balances of the Asian NIEs
Note: 12-month moving averages.
Source: Compiled by NRI based on customs statistics of individual countries.

first phase (the phase of a strengthening yen), which lasted from 1985 to 1986, the yen appreciated sharply against both the dollar and the NIEs' currencies (which remained broadly stable against the dollar). In the second phase (the phase of simultaneous appreciation of the yen and NIEs' currencies), which lasted from 1987 to 1988, both the yen and the NIEs' currencies appreciated sharply against the dollar (and the ASEAN's currencies), so that the yen stabilized against the NIEs' currencies. In the third phase (the phase of a weakening yen), lasting from early 1989 to mid-1990, the yen depreciated sharply not only against the NIEs' currencies (which had by then stabilized against the dollar), but also against the ASEAN's currencies. In the fourth phase, starting from mid-1990, the yen rebounded against the dollar as well as against all Asian currencies.

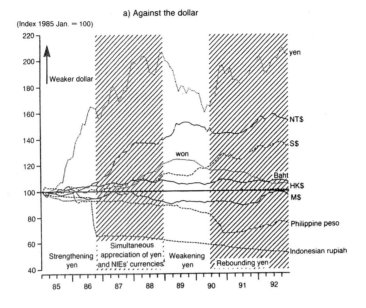

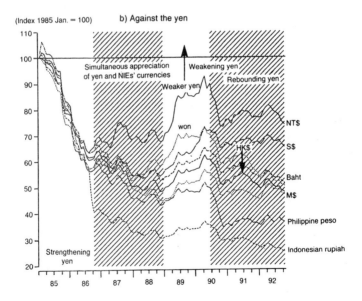

Figure 2.6 Exchange rates of the Asian currencies

Source: Compiled by NRI based on IMF, *International Financial Statistics* and official statistics.

The 'flying-geese pattern' of Pacific trade imbalances[9]

In the last section we examined how growing trade imbalances had affected the exchange rates of the Asian countries. In this section we study the feedback from exchange rate changes to the balance of trade – with emphasis on the trade balance between the two sides of the Pacific.

The US trade deficit dropped from $152 billion in 1987 to $66 billion in 1991, thanks mainly to the sharp fall of the dollar against other major currencies that began in 1985 (Table 2.3). By region, EC contributed $37 billion to the decline, followed by the Asian NIEs ($17 billion) and Japan ($13 billion). The narrowing of the US trade imbalance with Japan and the Asian NIEs, however, has been accompanied by a widening of the deficit with China and the ASEAN countries. As a result, the US deficit with Asia (Japan, the NIEs, ASEAN and China) in 1991 still reached $77 billion, surpassing the total US trade deficit of $66 billion.

The shifting of the source of increases in the US deficit in Asia from Japan to the Asian NIEs, and further to China and the ASEAN countries, has followed a 'flying-geese pattern' (Figure 2.7). In such a process, trade and investment are responsible for transmitting economic changes from the more advanced countries to the less developed ones.[10]

Japan has played a leader's role in this process. The sharp appreciation of the yen since 1985 helped reduce Japan's trade surplus with the United States from its peak level of $56.3 billion in 1987 to $43.4 billion in 1991 (according to US statistics). The reduction occurred not only through price effects on the demand side, but also by a sharp increase in outward foreign direct investment. Increases in overseas production, both in the United States and at offshore production bases, first in the Asian NIEs and subsequently in ASEAN and China, also helped suppress Japanese exports to the United States.

The sharp appreciation of the yen boosted the Asian NIEs' exports to, and thus their trade surplus with, the United States. By 1987, their joint surplus with the United States reached $34.1 billion (according to US statistics). The subsequent appreciation of the NIEs' currencies, however, reduced export competitiveness and promoted outward foreign direct investment in these countries. Manufacturers in Hong Kong started to make extensive use of southern China as an offshore production base for exports. They were followed by investors from Taiwan. At the same time, foreign direct investment from the Asian NIEs to the ASEAN countries also increased sharply, and some Japanese companies relocated part of their production capacity from the

Table 2.3 US trade balance with the Asian countries

	1980	1985	1986	1987	1988	1989	1990	1991	1992
NIEs	−3,037	−22,148	−27,846	−34,117	−28,214	−24,345	−19,839	−13,666	−13,792
Korea	429	−4,057	−6,374	−8,888	−8,873	−6,278	−4,081	−1,506	−2,043
Taiwan	−2,558	−11,696	−14,267	−17,209	−12,585	−12,978	−11,175	−9,845	−9,397
Hong Kong	−2,021	−5,610	−5,860	−5,871	−4,550	−3,431	−2,805	−1,146	−731
Singapore	1,112	−784	−1,345	−2,148	−2,206	−1,658	−1,778	−1,169	−1,687
ASEAN	na	−5,880	−4,477	−4,992	−5,678	−7,113	−6,497	−7,119	−10,817
Indonesia	na	−3,774	−2,366	−2,627	−2,092	−2,282	−1,444	−1,347	−1,750
Malaysia	na	−761	−691	−1,024	−1,550	−1,874	−1,847	−2,201	−3,931
Philippines	na	−766	−609	−665	−788	−866	−913	−1,203	−1,596
Thailand	na	−579	−811	−676	−1,248	−2,091	−2,293	−2,368	−3,540
China	2,697	−6	−1,665	−2,796	−3,490	−6,235	−10,431	−12,689	−18,260
Japan	−10,077	−46,152	−55,030	−56,326	−51,794	−49,059	−41,105	−43,436	−49,418
EC	na	−18,847	−22,601	−20,645	−9,184	1,133	6,252	16,728	8,965
Total	−31	−117,708	−138,309	−152,119	−118,526	−109,318	−101,010	−66,256	−84,501

Notes: 1 Figures in $, mil. 2 na: not available.
Source: US Department of Commerce.

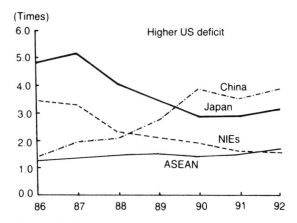

Figure 2.7 The Flying-geese pattern of Pacific trade imbalances
Note: US imports divided by US exports (manufactured goods only).
Source: Compiled by NRI based on US Department of Commerce, *US Foreign Trade Highlights*.

Asian NIEs to the ASEAN countries. Consequently, the trade surplus in 1991 of the four Asian NIEs with the United States was down 60 per cent from its 1987 peak, falling to $13.7 billion.

In contrast to trends in Japan and the Asian NIEs, the inflows of foreign direct investment into China and the ASEAN countries have boosted their exports to, and trade surpluses with, the United States.

Although the United States has reduced its trade deficit with Taiwan and Hong Kong in the last few years, the reduction has been accompanied by a rapid increase in the trade deficit with China. Indeed, the trade gap between the United States and China, Taiwan, and Hong Kong combined (or Greater China) has continued to rise. China's trade balance with the United States, which was more or less in balance in 1985, jumped to a surplus of $18.3 billion in 1992 (according to US statistics).[11] As a result, China has become the second largest source of the US trade deficit since 1991, behind only Japan.

The sharp increase in China's trade surplus with the United States largely reflects the large-scale relocation of the manufacturing sectors of Hong Kong, and to a lesser extent of Taiwan, into southern China. Indeed, the rapid increase in US-bound re-exports has been accompanied by an absolute decline in Hong Kong's domestic exports to the United States. Recently, an increasing number of Taiwanese companies have also been investing in southern China and this has also raised

China's exports to the United States (and thus its trade surplus with the United States) at Taiwan's expense.

Among China's leading export items to the United States, miscellaneous manufactured articles (textiles, garments, toys and footwear) have recorded the highest growth rates. In contrast, Hong Kong and Taiwan have reduced their exports of these products to the United States and raised their exports of capital and intermediate goods to China to support production there instead.

Against this background, trade friction between China and the United States has escalated. In its 'Foreign Trade Barriers' report published in late March 1991, the USTR criticized severely China's trade policy in areas ranging from import policies and export incentives to lack of intellectual property protection and barriers in services and investment. The United States demanded that China should improve its legal system to conform with international rules and that it abide by the rules faithfully. At the same time, it threatened to suspend China's most favoured nation (MFN) status and to cut the quotas of textile imports from China. In October 1991, the United States initiated a Section 301 case, which required China to satisfy American complaints within a year or face retaliation.

If economic relations between China and the United States deteriorate, Hong Kong and southern China would suffer most. As discussed above, recent increases in China's trade surplus with the United States have mainly reflected the surge in foreign direct investment in southern China by manufacturers from Hong Kong and Taiwan. A harsher US stance against China would not only harm the Hong Kong economy but also reduce the attractiveness of southern China as an offshore production base for multinationals, with adverse effect on China's open-door policy.

Boosted by strong exports of manufactured goods, the ASEAN countries' trade surplus with the United States rose from $4.5 billion in 1986 to $10.8 billion in 1992. The ASEAN countries are developing rapidly into offshore production bases for multinationals. Judging from the experiences of the Asian NIEs and China, further widening of their trade surpluses with the United States may intensify trade friction. Already, there has been rising pressure in the United States to abolish the GSP privileges of Malaysia and Thailand.

FOREIGN DIRECT INVESTMENT AND THE BALANCE OF PAYMENTS

The theoretical framework

The flow of foreign direct investment has become a major factor determining the flow of trade and thus trade imbalances in the Asia-Pacific region. Here, we ignore the presence of third countries and concentrate on the effect of foreign direct investment on the external balances of the investing and receiving countries. Because the impact on the investing country and the receiving country are the mirror image of each other, we proceed by focusing on the impact of the receiving country.[12]

The impact of foreign direct investment on the external balance of the receiving country (against the rest of the world) can be analysed at three levels – the trade balance, the current-account balance, and the capital-account balance.

The following four effects are important in determining the impact of an inflow in foreign direct investment on the (merchandise) trade account of the receiving country: the import-substitution effect, the export-expansion effect, the import-expansion effect and the export-substitution effect. The first two effects tend to improve the trade balance while the last two tend to worsen the trade balance. The size of each effect changes over time corresponding to different stages of the life cycle of the investment. This can be illustrated, for example, by considering a Japanese company building a petroleum refinery in Indonesia (Figure 2.8).

The import-substitution effect refers to the fall in Indonesian imports of refined petroleum with the expansion of domestic production. The positive effect on Indonesia's trade balance can only be realized after the plant is completed and production comes on stream (Figure 2.8a).

The export-expansion effect refers to the increase in exports when part of the output of the plant is exported. As in the case of the import substitution effect, the positive effect on the trade balance can only be realized after the plant is completed and production comes on stream (Figure 2.8b).

The import-expansion effect refers to the increase in imports to support production in the new plant. At the initial stage when the plant is under construction, this involves a substantial increase in the imports of capital goods and construction materials. At the later stage when the plant is completed, the bulk of imports shifts to intermediate goods, such as crude oil in this case (Figure 2.8c).

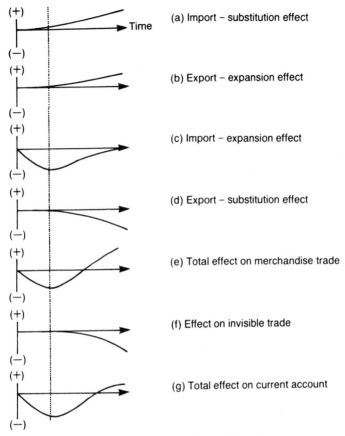

Figure 2.8 The J-curve effect of foreign direct investment
Source: NRI.

The export-substitution effect refers to the decline in Indonesian exports of raw or intermediate products (Indonesian crude petroleum), since they are retained as input for domestic use. Like the import-substitution effect and the export-expansion effect, the export-substitution effect on the trade balance only comes after the new plant begins production (Figure 2.8d).

These four effects combine to yield a J-curve pattern of the trade balance over time (Figure 2.8e). In the initial stage the import-expansion effect dominates so that the trade balance deteriorates. It is only after the new plant begins operating that the trade balance begins to improve. It takes even longer time for the trade balance to turn into a surplus.

To derive the impact on the current account, the invisible trade balance, which usually deteriorates with inflow of foreign direct investment, needs to be considered (Figure 2.8f). Major debit items within the invisible trade account include payments of investment income (both interest on borrowing and profit remittance), and various fees related to business services such as consulting, royalties and licensing.

The impact of an inflow of foreign direct investment on the current account of the receiving country can now be calculated by summing up the balances on the merchandise trade account and the invisible account (Figure 2.8g). The deficit in the services account tends to partly offset the positive effect (or aggravate the negative effect) of the trade balance on the current account. Still, the changes of the current account over time follows a J-curve pattern similar to that of the trade account – deteriorating in the initial stage when the plant is under construction and then improving as production comes on stream.

For the sake of completion, the overall balance can be derived by adding the capital account to the current account. The credit side of the capital account involves the receipt of loans and paid in capital from the parent company while the debit side mainly reflects loan repayments, and the remittance of paid-in capital when the business is sold or liquidated. In net terms, the capital account tends to be in surplus in the initial stage when the plant is under construction and in deficit in a later stage when repayment of debt begins.

The Asian experience

The development of the Asian NIEs, and later China and the ASEAN countries, into offshore production bases for multinationals has led to a surge in intra-regional trade. Exports from the investing countries to the host countries, composed largely of capital and intermediate goods, have surged, boosting (reducing) the trade surplus (deficit) of the former with the latter.

Japan's trade surplus with the Asian NIEs reached $46.5 billion in 1992, surpassing that with the United States ($43.7 billion), which has dominated Japan's trade surplus in the last ten years (Table 2.4). In contrast to the situation between 1986 and 1988, the recent round of increase in Japan's trade surplus with the Asian NIEs has not been accompanied by an increase in the latter's trade surplus with the United States. Instead, the worsening trade deficit with Japan has led to a sharp deterioration in the Asian NIEs' overall trade balance. Against this

Table 2.4 Japanese trade balance with the Asian countries

	1980	1985	1986	1987	1988	1989	1990	1991	1992
NIEs	11,820	12,654	17,544	20,644	24,811	25,602	30,719	39,540	46,490
Korea	2,372	3,005	5,183	5,154	3,631	3,567	5,751	7,729	6,190
Taiwan	2,852	1,640	3,161	4,218	5,611	6,442	6,933	8,762	11,709
Hong Kong	4,191	5,742	6,087	7,311	9,597	9,307	10,894	14,251	18,716
Singapore	2,404	2,267	3,113	3,961	5,972	6,287	7,137	8,799	9,874
ASEAN	−10,590	−9,411	−6,280	−6,822	−5,987	−5,126	−2,246	−1,507	572
Indonesia	−9,709	−7,947	−4,649	−5,437	−6,443	−7,720	−7,682	−7,157	−6,648
Malaysia	−1,410	−2,162	−2,137	−2,604	−1,650	−983	110	1,163	1,571
Philippines	−268	−307	−133	62	−304	321	347	308	1,218
Thailand	797	1,003	639	1,157	2,410	3,256	4,979	4,179	4,431
China	755	5,995	4,204	848	−383	−2,630	−5,924	−5,523	−4,989
USA	6,959	39,485	51,401	52,089	47,597	44,943	37,954	38,220	43,674
EC	8,808	11,124	16,686	20,024	22,802	19,761	18,490	27,365	31,184
Total	−10,721	46,099	82,743	79,706	77,563	64,328	52,149	77,789	107,064

Notes: 1 Figures in $, mil.
Source: Japanese Ministry of Finance.

background, trade friction between Japan and the Asian NIEs, particularly South Korea and Taiwan, has intensified.

Japan has traditionally run a substantial trade deficit with the ASEAN countries, reflecting its dependence on Malaysia and Indonesia as major suppliers of oil, but the large inflow of foreign direct investment from the former to the latter in the last few years has changed the picture. Rising Japanese exports of capital and intermediate goods to the ASEAN countries to support offshore production activities there has led to a surge in Japanese exports to these countries since 1987. As a result, Japan's trade balance with the ASEAN countries which recorded a $9.4 billion deficit in 1985 turned into a surplus of $0.6 billion in 1992. As more and more facilities invested in these countries in the last few years come on stream, the need to import parts and components from Japan will increase further over the next few years.

The Asian NIEs' trade with its developing neighbours has also come to be dominated by the flow of foreign direct investment. Taiwan, by far the largest source of foreign direct investment among the Asian NIEs, for example, has increased its trade surpluses with China and the ASEAN countries. Indeed, reflecting the surge in Taiwan's indirect exports to China, Hong Kong has replaced Japan as Taiwan's second largest export destination since 1990, only after the United States. Also, Taiwan has run a larger trade surplus with Hong Kong than with the United States since 1991. Taiwan's trade balance with the ASEAN countries has also turned from a deficit to a surplus.

3

EXCHANGE-RATE REALIGNMENT AND SHORT-TERM ECONOMIC FLUCTUATIONS

INTRODUCTION[1]

The Asia-Pacific region has been the fastest growing part of the world economy throughout the postwar period. Rapid economic growth, however, does not necessarily imply stable growth (Figure 3.1). Korean economic growth, for example, has fluctuated between 4.7 per cent (1992) and 13.0 per cent (1987) since 1985; Malaysian economic growth, meanwhile, has oscillated between −1.1 per cent (1985) to 9.8 per cent (1990). In this chapter, fluctuations in exchange rates, the yen–dollar rate in particular, are identified as the major factors contributing to swings in economic activity in the Asian countries. We find that an appreciation of the yen tends to raise economic growth in the Asian NIEs but lower that in the ASEAN countries. This asymmetry reflects differences in their trade structures and the resulting differences in their relations with Japan. In the first part of this chapter we review the macroeconomic performance of the Asian countries since 1985, with emphasis on the impact of exchange-rate realignment. In the second half we focus on the relationship between the yen–dollar rate and short-term economic growth in the Asian countries.

MACROECONOMIC PERFORMANCE SINCE 1985

The Asian economies have passed through four phases since 1985 when we examine the relationship between the economic growth rates of the Asian NIEs (North) and the ASEAN countries (South) – the phase of diverging growth rates (1985-86), the phase of converging growth rates (1987–88), the phase of reversal of North-South growth rates (1989 to mid-1990), and the phase since mid-1990 when the Asian NIEs have regained their lead over ASEAN. These four phases correspond broadly

41

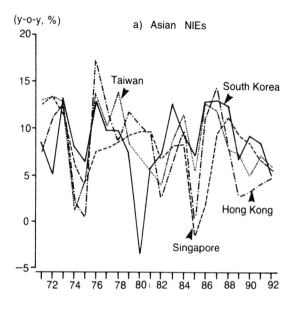

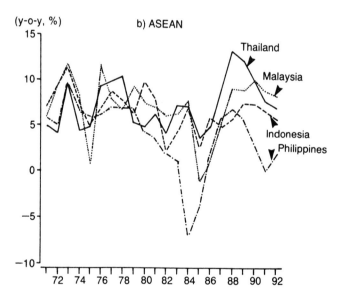

Figure 3.1 Economic growth of the Asian countries
Source: Compiled by NRI based on IMF, *International Financial Statistics* and official statistics.

to the four phases of exchange-rate realignment discussed in the last chapter, suggesting that currency fluctuations have been a dominant factor determining economic growth in the Asian NIEs and the ASEAN countries.

The phase of a strengthening yen (1985–6)

The period between 1985–6 was characterized by the divergence of economic growth rates between the Asian NIEs and the ASEAN countries, reflecting the sharp appreciation of the yen and a slump in commodity prices (oil prices in particular). The Asian NIEs were the major beneficiaries of the yen's appreciation and lower oil prices. Being importers of oil and exporters of manufactured goods, their terms of trade improved substantially. On the demand side, this boosted consumption as real incomes rose. On the supply side, the improvement in the terms of trade raised export profits. The yen's appreciation also made their exports more competitive on international markets, and many Japanese manufacturers invested in the Asian NIEs to take advantage of lower labour costs. With the recession in 1985 just over, unemployment rates were relatively high and upward pressures on wages were minimal. Against this background, all of the Asian NIEs except Singapore recorded admirable growth rates in 1986.

In contrast to the Asian NIEs, the ASEAN countries plunged into a recession in 1985–6. For the ASEAN countries, lower commodity prices meant a deterioration in their balance of payments and a reduction in government revenues. Governments in these countries were forced to implement austerity measures to curb domestic demand, with adverse effects on economic growth. At this stage, the yen's appreciation did not benefit the ASEAN countries much in terms of competitiveness because primary commodities rather than manufactured products made up the bulk of their exports. On the contrary, the stronger yen actually added to the ASEAN countries' debt servicing costs, since a large portion of their outstanding debt was denominated in yen. Unlike the Asian NIEs, which are more dependent on the United States as an export market, the ASEAN countries were also adversely affected by the economic slowdown in Japan, which absorbed one-quarter of their exports.

As a result of these trends, the Asian NIEs' economic growth rate reached 11.9 per cent in 1986, far exceeding ASEAN's growth rate of 3.4 per cent. Indeed, economic growth rates in the Asia-Pacific region declined steadily moving from the North to the South. Among the four NIEs, Korea, Taiwan and Hong Kong grew at double-digit rates, but

Singapore, whose economy is closely integrated with those of its ASEAN neighbours, remained mired in the doldrums.

The phase of simultaneous appreciation of the yen and NIEs' currencies (1987–8)

Between 1987 and 1988, the pattern of economic growth in the Asia-Pacific region shifted from diverging growth rates between countries in the North and those in the South to converging North-South growth rates. This reflected not only the turnaround in commodity prices, but, more importantly, currency appreciation in the Asian NIEs.

Against the backdrop of burgeoning trade imbalances, the Asian NIEs' trade friction with the United States escalated, and in 1986 the United States began to pressure them to revalue their currencies. At the same time, with unemployment rates falling to historically low levels, a wage-price spiral began to plague the NIEs' economies. Currency appreciation, coupled with rising wages, led to a sharp deterioration in their export competitiveness, and their attractiveness as offshore production bases declined. Japanese multinationals began to shift their direct investment to the ASEAN countries in 1987 (Table 3.1). They were followed by manufacturers in the Asian NIEs themselves, who had been granted more freedom to invest abroad as the national current accounts moved into surplus. Against this background, export growth in the Asian NIEs (in dollar terms) decelerated from 34 per cent in 1987 to 26 per cent in 1988 (Figure 3.2). Constrained by the slowdown in export growth, the economic growth rate of the Asian NIEs dropped to 9.8 per cent in 1988 from 12.4 per cent in 1987.

To cope with the changing economic environment, the Asian NIEs have expended much energy in restructuring their economies. This has resulted in a shift of the engine of economic growth from net exports to domestic demand, and a more balanced export structure in terms of both geographical and commodity composition.

Among the recent structural changes in the Asian NIEs, the progress made in market diversification has been the most remarkable. With protectionism in the United States mounting and the prospects for the US economy becoming more and more uncertain, particularly after the stock market crash of October 1987, the Asian NIEs made stringent efforts to promote exports to other markets. In addition to exports to Japan and the EC, intra-regional trade among the Asian NIEs themselves also expanded sharply. Japan-bound exports surged 50 per cent in 1987 and 33 per cent in 1988 (based on Japanese customs

Table 3.1 Japanese investment in the Asian countries

Fiscal Year	1985		1986		1987		1988		1989		1990		1991		1992	
	$, mil.	% share	$, mil.	% share	$, mil.	% share	$, mil.	% share	$, mil.	% share	$, mil.	% share	$, mil.	% share	$, mil.	% share
Asian NIEs	718	5.9	1,531	6.9	2,580	7.7	3,264	6.9	4,900	7.3	3,355	5.9	2,203	5.3	1,922	5.6
South Korea	134	1.1	436	2.0	647	1.9	483	1.0	606	0.9	284	0.5	260	0.6	225	0.7
Taiwan	114	0.9	291	1.3	367	1.1	372	0.8	494	0.7	446	0.8	405	1.0	292	0.9
Hong Kong	131	1.1	502	2.2	1,072	3.2	1,662	3.5	1,898	2.8	1,785	3.1	925	2.2	735	2.2
Singapore	339	2.8	302	1.4	494	1.5	747	1.6	1,902	2.8	840	1.5	613	1.5	670	2.0
ASEAN	596	4.9	553	2.5	1,030	3.1	1,966	4.2	2,782	4.1	3,242	5.7	3,083	7.4	3,197	9.4
Indonesia	408	3.3	250	1.1	545	1.6	586	1.2	631	0.9	1,105	1.9	1,193	2.9	1,676	4.9
Malaysia	79	0.6	158	0.7	163	0.5	387	0.8	673	1.0	725	1.3	880	2.1	704	2.1
Philippines	61	0.5	21	0.1	72	0.2	134	0.3	202	0.3	258	0.5	203	0.5	160	0.5
Thailand	48	0.4	124	0.6	250	0.7	859	1.8	1,276	1.9	1,154	2.0	807	1.9	657	1.9
China	100	0.8	226	1.0	1,226	3.7	296	0.6	438	0.6	349	0.6	579	1.4	1,070	3.1
USA	5,395	44.2	10,165	45.5	14,704	44.1	21,701	46.2	32,540	48.2	26,128	45.9	18,026	43.3	13,819	40.5
Europe	1,930	15.8	3,469	15.5	6,575	19.7	9,116	19.4	14,808	21.9	14,294	25.1	9,371	22.5	7,061	20.7
World total	12,217	100.0	22,320	100.0	33,364	100.0	47,022	100.0	67,540	100.0	56,911	100.0	41,584	100.0	34,138	100.0

Source: Japanese Ministry of Finance.

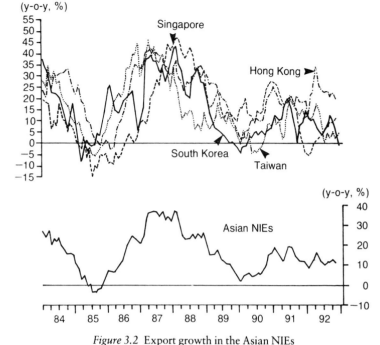

Figure 3.2 Export growth in the Asian NIEs
Note: Dollar-based 3-month moving averages.
Source: Compiled by NRI based on customs statistics of individual countries.

statistics). As a result, the rising trend of the Asian NIEs' dependence on the US market was reversed in 1987, while dependence on Japan, the EC and other Asian NIEs increased.

At the same time, the Asian NIEs have striven to improve their productivity and upgrade their industries by investing heavily in new plant and equipment and importing foreign technology. Technology-intensive industries (particularly electronics and automobiles) have grown rapidly, replacing textiles as the leading growth sector. More and more manufacturers in structurally-declining industries have started to shift their operations to the ASEAN countries and to China. Manufacturers based in Hong Kong have been actively subcontracting part of their production to factories in neighbouring provinces of southern China. Taiwan has also emerged as a major investor in the ASEAN countries and southern China.

The adverse effects of the slowdown in export growth on economic expansion were partly offset by robust growth in domestic demand.

Fuelled by increases in jobs and wages, consumption picked up, and business spending on new plant and equipment firmed. In the case of Taiwan, whose currency had appreciated most sharply against the US dollar among the Asian NIEs, the strengthening of domestic demand helped to sustain moderate economic growth. Following in Taiwan's footsteps, South Korea's pattern of economic growth also shifted from one led by net exports to one led by domestic demand in 1989.

In contrast to the Asian NIEs, the ASEAN countries benefited from the new economic environment. Since they were less vulnerable to pressure from the United States to revalue their exchange rates, their currencies remained undervalued. This, coupled with stable wages, made them more attractive in the eyes of foreign multinationals as sites for production facilities. In fact, Japanese investment in the ASEAN countries jumped by 83 per cent in 1987, followed by a 91 per cent leap in 1988. The recovery coincided with a major shift in the ASEAN countries' development policies from import substitution to export promotion.

In the past, foreign direct investment in the ASEAN countries was concentrated in natural-resource development, but recently it has shifted to the manufacturing sector. In addition to Japan, the Asian NIEs have grown in importance as investors in this region. Much of the investment was at first concentrated in Thailand, but gradually it spread to Malaysia, Indonesia and the Philippines as well. Led by manufactured exports, the ASEAN economies recovered from the doldrums in 1987. Consequently, the economic growth rates of the Asian NIEs and the ASEAN countries converged, with the gap between the two shrinking from 8.5 per cent in 1986 to 1.9 per cent in 1988.

The phase of a weakening yen (1989 to mid-1990)

The Asian currencies appreciated sharply against the yen between early 1989 and mid-1990, although they stabilized against the dollar. During this period, the Asian NIEs' export competitiveness continued to deteriorate, and their attractiveness in the eyes of multinationals as offshore production bases waned.

The yen's depreciation exacerbated the downward trend in export growth in the Asian NIEs that had been going on since early 1988. The NIEs are major exporters of manufactured goods, placing them in direct competition with Japan. Appreciation of the local currencies against the yen dampens exports, both by making them more expensive in Japan (which has grown in importance as an export market) and by reducing their price competitiveness against Japanese products in the United States and other major markets.

Over the above period, Japanese export competitiveness recovered alongside the yen's depreciation, and the outflow of Japanese direct investment in search of lower production costs began to show signs of peaking out. In particular, Japanese investment in Korea and Taiwan stagnated. At the same time, Japanese investment in the Asian NIEs shifted from the manufacturing sector to such service industries as retailing and distribution. For Japanese multinationals, the role of the Asian NIEs began to shift from offshore production bases to export markets.

In addition to the exchange-rate factor, the Asian NIEs faced other difficulties at this time. Inflation continued to follow an upward trend, mainly reflecting surging wages. Consumer prices rose by 10.1 per cent in Hong Kong and 4.4 per cent in Taiwan in 1989, reaching their highest levels since the second oil crisis of the early 1980s. South Korea had to cope with the aftermath of the Seoul Olympics. Hong Kong suffered a major blow from the Tiananmen Square incident in China, and the economy plunged into a recession that saw economic growth fall to 2.8 per cent in 1989. In contrast, the Singapore economy remained strong, thanks to its close ties with the booming ASEAN economies.

The ASEAN countries were less adversely affected by the yen's depreciation because their currencies remained substantially under-valued. They also benefited from some diversion of foreign direct investment by multinationals from China. The inflow of foreign direct investment from both Japan and the Asian NIEs stayed at a high level, and the ASEAN countries maintained moderate export growth. Indonesia and Malaysia, which have large yen-denominated debt, also benefited from a reduction in their debt burden.

Reflecting these developments, economic growth in 1989 reached 8.3 per cent in the ASEAN countries but dropped to 6.1 per cent in the Asian NIEs. It was the first time since the second oil crisis of 1980 that economic growth in the ASEAN countries had surpassed that in the Asian NIEs – a trend which continued into 1990 (Figure 3.3). At the same time, the traditional pattern of economic growth in the Asia-Pacific region characterized by high growth rates in countries in the North and low growth rates in countries in the South gave way to one characterized by the reversal of North-South growth rates (Figure 3.4).

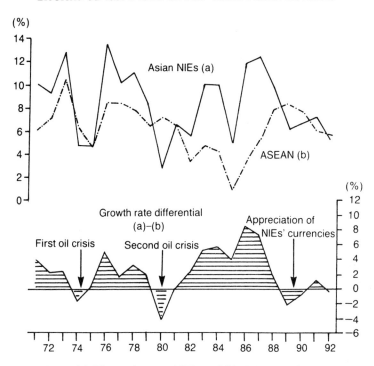

Figure 3.3 The gap between NIEs' and ASEAN's growth rates
Source: Compiled by NRI based on IMF, *International Financial Statistics* and official statistics.

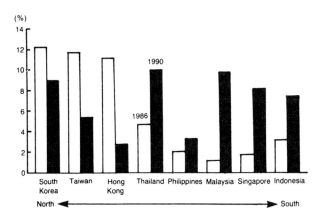

Figure 3.4 Converging growth rates between North and South
Source: Compiled by NRI based on IMF, *International Financial Statistics* and official statistics.

The phase of a rebounding yen (mid-1990–1991)

The pendulum began to swing back to the North in the second half of 1990, thanks to the rebound of the yen against the dollar, and a recovery in the Chinese economy. The Asian NIEs bottomed out, reflecting stronger exports, while the ASEAN economies started to decelerate as their governments tightened monetary policy to cool down overheated economic growth. The slowdown in economic growth in the industrial countries, which became apparent in the United States and Europe in the second half of 1990 and in Japan in early 1991, however, reduced the average growth rate of the Asian NIEs and ASEAN to 6.8 per cent in 1991 and further to 5.3 per cent in 1992, its lowest level since 1985.

In the Asian NIEs, exports began to recover in mid-1990, bolstered by a higher yen, surging orders from the unified Germany and an economic recovery in China. The slack created by negative growth in exports to the United States was picked up by the surge in exports to Europe and intra-regional trade. Hong Kong and Taiwan, in particular, benefited from the booming economic activities in southern China. The firming of exports offset the slowdown in domestic demand, sustaining economic growth at a moderate level.

In contrast, the ASEAN countries entered a phase of adjustment in 1991 after three years of rapid growth. In addition to sluggish growth in overseas markets, the monetary tightening to cope with deteriorating current account balances (which surged to historically high levels) and rising domestic inflation (which reached its highest level since the second oil crisis) imposed a further drag on the ASEAN economies. Domestic demand, in particular, decelerated on the back of rising interest rates. The inflow of foreign direct investment, which has boosted the ASEAN economies in the last few years, also peaked out. As a result, the Asian NIEs regained their lead over the ASEAN countries in 1991, with economic growth in the former recovering to 7.2 per cent (from 6.6 per cent in 1990) and that in the latter declining to 6.0 per cent (from 7.7 per cent a year earlier).

THE IMPACT OF FLUCTUATIONS IN THE YEN–DOLLAR RATE

So far we have examined how the global exchange-rate realignment since 1985 has affected macroeconomic performance in the Asian countries. Here, we look more closely at the impact of the fluctuations in the yen–dollar rate on economic growth in these countries.

The yen–dollar rate has become a major determinant of the level of economic activity in the countries in Asia since 1985. A comparison of past trends in the yen–dollar rate and the average growth rate of the Asian NIEs depicts a very close relationship between them, with economic growth accelerating as the yen appreciates (see Figure 1.5). Indeed, the Asian NIEs' economic growth rate is even more highly correlated with the yen–dollar rate than with the US economic growth rate, which is usually considered to have the dominant effect on these economies. The relationship between the yen–dollar rate and the growth rates of the ASEAN countries is less obvious, but our analysis suggests that, in contrast to the Asian NIEs, a stronger yen tends to lower economic growth in the ASEAN countries. This asymmetry reflects differences in their trade structures and the resulting differences in their trade relations with Japan.

Theoretical analysis

The relationship between the yen–dollar rate and economic growth in the Asian NIEs is summarized conceptually in Figure 3.5a. Being small, open economies, with export structures resembling that of Japan, they compete with Japan in international markets. Their *export prices* are

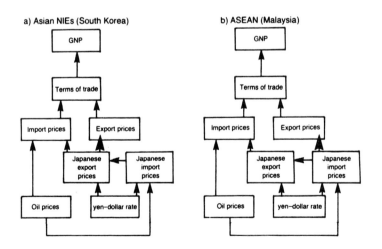

Figure 3.5 Models of GNP determination for the Asian countries
Note: Oil prices and import-export prices are measured in dollar terms.
Source: NRI.

51

largely determined by *Japanese export prices*, while their imports are dominated by primary commodities (particularly oil). Appreciation of the yen against the dollar raises Japanese export prices in dollar terms; manufacturers in the Asian NIEs, acting as price-takers in international markets, raise the prices of their exports as well. Although appreciation of the yen also raises the Asian NIEs' import prices (as Japan provides one-quarter of their imports), it is the effect on export prices that predominates, and the Asian NIEs' terms of trade improve as a result. In contrast, an increase in oil prices raises import prices more than export prices and leads to a deterioration in the Asian NIEs' terms of trade.

In contrast to the Asian NIEs, the ASEAN countries have trade structures complementary to that of Japan: the composition of their exports resembles the import composition rather than the export composition of Japan; the composition of their imports, meanwhile, resembles that of Japanese exports. As a result, the ASEAN countries' *export prices* follow closely the movement of *Japanese import prices* (Figure 3.5b). When the yen appreciates, export growth in Japan slows down, dragging down the demand for, and thus the import prices of, primary commodities. This in turn imposes downward pressure on the export prices of the ASEAN countries. At the same time, an appreciation of the yen drives up Japanese export prices and thus the import prices of the ASEAN countries, which depend heavily on Japan as their major source of capital goods. As a result, the ASEAN countries' terms of trade deteriorate. Also in contrast to the Asian NIEs, an increase in oil prices improves the ASEAN countries' terms of trade.

The terms of trade in turn play a dominant role in determining the GNP levels of both the Asian NIEs and the ASEAN countries (see Appendix at the end of this chapter for a theoretical analysis of the relationship between the terms of trade and GNP). With production heavily dependent on imported intermediate goods and capital equipment, the cost of imports forms the dominant part of input costs. An increase in import prices therefore raises the cost of production. On the other hand, as the bulk of production (particularly in the manufacturing sector) is for sale in overseas markets, export prices correspond broadly to output prices. An improvement (a deterioration) in the terms of trade boosts (lowers) profits and the level of production.

Taken together, a stronger yen tends to raise GNP in the Asian NIEs through improving their terms of trade while reducing GNP in the ASEAN countries through depressing their terms of trade. This asymmetry largely reflects differences between the trade structures of the Asian NIEs and the ASEAN countries, which to a large extent determine their trade relations with Japan. The more a country's trade structure resembles (complements) that of Japan, the more it benefits (suffers) from a stronger yen.

Empirical analysis

We can confirm the relationship between the yen–dollar rate and GNP swings in the Asian countries by estimating real GNP for individual countries using the yen–dollar rate and a time trend (as a proxy for productivity growth). We also include oil prices as an explanatory variable in the case of Malaysia and Indonesia, the two major oil exporters in the region. The result, as summarized in Table 3.2, supports our hypothesis that the yen–dollar rate is a major determinant of GNP swings in the Asian countries. A stronger yen tends to boost economic

Table 3.2 Estimation of GNP of individual Asian countries

| GNP | Independent variables | | | $\bar{R}^2$ | D.W. |
	Time	¥–$ rate	Oil prices		
South Korea	0.0690 (17.47)	−0.2600 (−3.27)		0.989	0.792
Taiwan	0.0751 (36.53)	−0.1733 (−4.18)	–	0.997	1.349
Hong Kong	0.0782 (18.48)	−0.0639 (−0.75)	–	0.988	0.915
Singapore	0.0756 (23.23)	0.1230 (1.18)	–	0.990	0.903
Indonesia	0.0539 (19.03)	0.0111 (0.27)	0.0561 (5.00)	0.995	1.588
Malaysia	0.0588 (14.31)	0.1056 (1.75)	0.0528 (3.24)	0.990	1.282
Philippines	0.0386 (5.20)	0.1490 (1.00)	–	0.802	0.285
Thailand	0.0621 (24.72)	−0.0933 (−1.84)	–	0.993	0.763

Notes: 1 Sample period: 1972–89 (annual rate). 2 Figures in ( ) denote t-values. 3 Except for time trend, all variables are in log form so that the coefficients correspond to elasticities.
Source: NRI.

growth in South Korea, Taiwan, Hong Kong and Thailand and depress it in Malaysia, Singapore, Indonesia and the Philippines.

As explained above, this asymmetry is closely related to differences in trade structures between these countries. The more (less) competitive a country's manufacturing sector is in international markets, the more it competes with Japan, and the more it benefits (suffers) from a stronger yen. This relation is shown in Figure 3.6, where we plot, for eight Asian countries, the elasticities of GNP with respect to the yen–dollar rate (as estimated in Table 3.2) against the respective specialization indexes of manufactured goods. The latter measures the competitiveness of these countries' manufactured goods in international markets.

The relationship between the yen–dollar rate and GNP in the Asian NIEs can be tested in more detail using Korean data (Table 3.3). For the sake of comparison, Korean GNP is first estimated using a time trend (first equation), and then other explanatory variables are added. In line with our model, the result shows that a 1.0 per cent depreciation (appreciation) of the yen against the dollar tends to reduce (raise) Korean GNP by 0.14 per cent, while a 1.0 per cent increase (decrease) in oil prices tends to reduce (raise) Korean GNP by 0.16 per cent (second

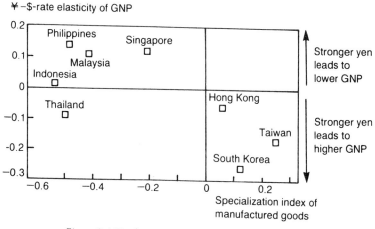

Figure 3.6 Trade structure and the ¥ /$ elasticity of GNP

Notes: 1 ¥ –$ rate elasticity of GNP = % change in GNP/% change in ¥ –$ rate. Figures are obtained from Table 3.2.

2 Specialization index of manufactured goods = $\dfrac{\text{Exports} - \text{Imports of manufactured goods}}{\text{Exports} + \text{Imports of manufactured goods}}$

3 Figures are averages of 1972 and 1988.

Source: NRI.

Table 3.3 Estimation of Korean GNP

Dependent variables	Independent variables				$\bar{R}^2$	D.W.
	Time	Oil prices	¥–$ rate	Terms of trade		
GNP	0.0183 (38.79)	–	–	–	0.964	0.372
GNP	0.0184 (36.48)	−0.1626 (−10.02)	−0.1418 (−5.00)	–	0.991	2.134
GNP	0.0163 (60.17)	–	–	0.7425 (14.57)	0.991	1.836

Notes: 1 Sample period: 77Q3–90Q1. GNP figures are seasonally adjusted. 2 Figures in ( ) denote t-values. 3 Except for time trend, all variables are in log form so that the coefficients correspond to elasticities. 4 Shiller lags of appropriate length used in estimation and figures show cumulative effect.
Source: NRI.

equation). At the same time, a 1.0 per cent improvement (deterioration) in the terms of trade tends to raise (reduce) Korean GNP by 0.74 per cent (third equation). In both the second and third equations, the t-values of the relevant variables are significant at the 99 per cent confidence level and both the R^2 and D.W. statistics improve over the case when only a time trend is included in the estimation.

Korea's import–export prices and terms of trade can be estimated using combinations of a time trend, oil prices, the yen–dollar rate and Japanese export prices (Table 3.4). In all cases, the independent variables are statistically significant (at the 99 per cent confidence level) in explaining the dependent variables and all the regression coefficients carry the expected signs. In particular, Korea's export prices are highly correlated with Japanese export prices, which in turn follow closely movements in the yen–dollar rate. A 1.0 per cent depreciation of the yen against the dollar, for example, is estimated to reduce Japanese export prices by 0.63 per cent and Korean export prices by 0.46 per cent. At the same time, it also reduces Korean import prices by 0.28 per cent.

Taken together, a 1.0 per cent depreciation (appreciation) of the yen is estimated to reduce (raise) Korea's terms of trade by 0.19 per cent. This, together with the last equation in Table 3.3, implies that a 1.0 per cent depreciation (appreciation) of the yen against the dollar tends to lower (raise) Korean GNP by 0.14 per cent (0.19×0.74). This is consistent with the result obtained by estimating Korean GNP directly

Table 3.4 Estimation of Korean import-export prices and terms of trade

Dependent variables	Independent variables				$\bar{R}^2$	D.W.
	Time	Oil prices	¥-$ rate	Japanese export prices		
Export prices	0.0006 (1.00)	0.1539 (7.63)	−0.4637 (−13.14)	–	0.950	0.520
Export prices	–	–	–	0.8567 (30.78)	0.951	0.386
Import prices	−0.0026 (−4.31)	0.3937 (20.27)	−0.2765 (−8.14)	–	0.949	0.773
Import prices	−0.0294 (−4.66)	0.3288 (15.49)	–	0.4888 (8.10)	0.942	0.656
Terms of trade	0.0032 (5.83)	−0.2398 (−13.45)	−0.1872 (−6.01)	–	0.902	1.319
Terms of trade	0.0030 (5.78)	−0.2945 (−16.79)	–	0.3354 (6.72)	0.909	1.412
Reference: Japanese Export prices	−0.0008 (−2.97)	0.1595 (19.59)	−0.6346 (−44.58)	–	0.993	1.211

Notes: 1 Sample period: 77Q3–90Q1. 2 Figures in ( ) denote t-values. 3 Except for time trend, all variables are in log form so that the coefficients correspond to elasticities.
4 Shiller lags of appropriate length used in estimation and figures show cumulative effect.
Source: NRI.

using the yen–dollar rate (second equation in Table 3.3).

Our analysis suggests that the ups and downs of the Korean economy mainly reflect fluctuations in the yen–dollar rate and oil prices (Figure 3.7). Whereas the recession in 1979 and 1980 coincided with the second oil crisis, sluggish growth in the early 1980s can be attributed to the strengthening dollar (or the weakening yen). The situation was reversed in 1986–88, when the yen's appreciation led to a boom in the Korean economy. The deceleration in economic growth after 1989 again coincided with a rebound of the dollar against the yen.

Likewise, the relationship between the yen–dollar rate and income fluctuations in the ASEAN countries can be tested in more detail using data for Malaysia (Table 3.5). As in the case of Korea, the terms of trade

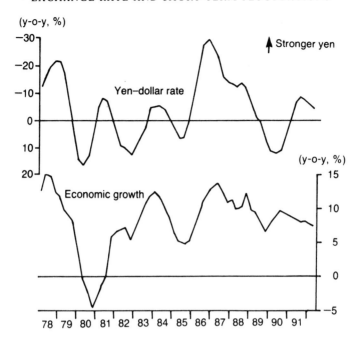

Figure 3.7 The yen–dollar rate and Korean economic growth
Note: 4-quarter moving averages.
Source: NRI.

have a significant impact on Malaysia's output level, with a 1.0 per cent improvement in the terms of trade driving up GNP by 0.29 per cent (last equation). In contrast to the Korean case, however, a 1.0 per cent depreciation of the yen and a 1.0 per cent increase in oil prices are estimated to raise Malaysian GNP by 0.11 per cent and 0.05 per cent respectively (second equation).

The result of estimating Malaysia's import-export prices and terms of trade is summarized in Table 3.6. In line with our prediction, Malaysian export prices are found to rise with oil prices and Japanese import prices, while import prices follow movement in oil prices and Japanese export prices. Reflecting the fact that a weaker yen raises Malaysia's export prices and reduces its import prices, the country's terms of trade improve as the yen depreciates. This contrasts sharply with the impact on the Asian NIEs' terms of trade. Because Malaysia is a net oil exporter, its terms of trade improve when oil prices rise.

Table 3.5 Estimation of Malaysian GNP

Dependent variables	Independent variables				$\bar{R}^2$	D.W.
	Time	*Oil prices*	*¥–$ rate*	*Terms of trade*		
GNP	0.0613 (28.89)	–	–	–	0.981	0.502
GNP	0.0588 (14.31)	0.0528 (3.24)	0.1056 (1.75)	–	0.990	1.282
GNP	0.0603 (45.39)	–	–	0.2877 (5.17)	0.993	0.862

Notes: 1 sample period: 1972–89 (annual data). 2 Figures in ( ) denote t-values. 3 Except for time trend, all variables are in log form so that the coefficients correspond to elasticities.
Source: NRI.

Concluding remarks

In this way, with interdependence in the Asia-Pacific region deepening, fluctuations in the yen–dollar rate have become a dominant factor contributing to swings in economic activity in Japan's neighbours. For the sake of macroeconomic stability, policymakers in these countries should pay more attention to the yen–dollar rate when formulating economic policy. As we shall see in Chapter 4, it may be desirable for some Asian countries to shift their current exchange-rate policy of pegging loosely to the dollar to pegging to the yen (or to a basket of currencies in which the yen carries a substantial weight). At the same time, stability in the yen–dollar rate and oil prices are desirable, and it would be in the interests of the Asian countries to participate directly in international forums of policy-coordination that go beyond the G-7 and OPEC.

With the ASEAN countries transforming themselves from exporters of primary commodities into exporters of manufactured goods, a change is also in store for their economic relations with Japan. The impact of the yen–dollar rate on these countries will become similar to that on the Asian NIEs. In the future, a stronger yen will boost economic growth in the ASEAN countries as it now does in the Asian NIEs.

The growing importance of the ASEAN countries as offshore production bases for Japanese manufacturers suggests that foreign direct investment will become more and more important as a channel

Table 3.6 Estimation of Malaysian import-export prices and terms of trade

Dependent variables	Independent variables					$\bar{R}^2$	D.W.
	Time	Oil prices	¥–$ rate	Japanese export prices	Japanese import prices		
Export prices	–	0.5216 (11.40)	0.5023 (3.35)	–	–	0.896	1.556
Export prices	–0.0442 (–5.70)	–	–	–	1.2838 (13.84)	0.946	1.632
Import prices	–	0.2893 (11.05)	–	0.6397 (3.63)	–	0.942	2.134
Terms of trade	–	0.1269 (3.76)	0.2298 (2.08)	–	–	0.418	1.219
Reference:							
Japanese export prices	–	0.1731 (17.21)	–0.5276 (–15.99)	–	–	0.988	1.852
Japanese import prices	0.0234 (2.19)	0.4352 (10.25)	0.2734 (1.74)	–	–	0.964	2.157

Notes: 1 Sample period: 1972–89 (annual data). 2 Figures in ( ) denote t-values. 3 Except for time trend, all variables are in log form so that the coefficients correspond to elasticities.
Source: NRI.

through which the effect of fluctuations in the yen–dollar rate will be transmitted to these countries. A stronger yen tends to raise Japanese investment in both the Asian NIEs and the ASEAN countries. Larger inflows of foreign direct investment in turn boost GNP by expanding production capacity. This contrasts with the effect through the terms of trade, which affects the Asian NIEs and the ASEAN countries asymmetrically. An appreciation of the yen tends to raise GNP in the Asian NIEs by raising both the terms of trade and foreign direct investment. In the case of the ASEAN countries, however, these two channels induce different effects, which tend to offset one another. The combined effect is less clear-cut.

APPENDIX: THE TERMS OF TRADE AND SHORT-TERM ECONOMIC FLUCTUATIONS

The relationship between the terms of trade and GNP for a small open economy can be examined using the following simple model[2].

Consider a small open economy that produces a final good Q with the input of domestically-owned capital K and labour L, and an imported intermediate good M. We assume that the host country is completely specialized in the production and consumption of Q, so that Q is also the only good exported. For simplicity, we also assume that M is the only good imported. The production process may be divided conceptually into two stages as follows[3]

$$
\begin{array}{l}
(K, L) \text{———————} Y \\
\qquad\qquad\qquad\qquad \backslash \\
Y = F(K, L) \qquad\qquad \text{———————} Q \\
\qquad\qquad\qquad / \\
\qquad\qquad M \qquad Q = \min(Y, M/m)
\end{array}
$$

Capital and labour are first combined to produce our national product Y, which is then combined with imported M to produce Q. K, L, and Y are related through the production function

$$Y = F(K, L), \quad F_L > 0, \quad F_{LL} < 0$$

while Q is produced by combining Y and M in fixed production. That is,

$$Q = \min(Y, M/m).$$

The last equation shows that the production of one unit of Q requires the input of (with appropriate choice of unit) one unit of Y and m units of the imported intermediate good.

Let P, W and E denote the nominal prices in domestic currency units of Q, L and foreign exchange (P, W and E will be referred to as the price level, nominal wage rate and exchange rate respectively), and P^* the nominal price of the intermediate input in terms of foreign-currency units. By the small-country assumption, P^* is exogenously given. The price of the intermediate input in terms of domestic-currency units is given by EP^* and the terms of trade (T) is given by P/EP^*. Since Q is the only final good consumed, P can be interpreted as the consumer price index. This should be distinguished from the GNP deflator, which is given by $P-mEP^*$. Likewise, two separate concepts of the real wage rate should be distinguished from one another. The first one is the product wage, defined as nominal wage rate deflated by the GNP deflator; that is, $W/(P-mEP^*)$. The second one is the real wage, defined as the nominal wage deflated by the consumer price index; that is, W/P.

Profit is defined as total income net of labour costs and the cost of the intermediate input. That is

$$\pi = PQ - WL - mEP^*Q.$$

From the production function, this can be written as

$$\pi = (P - mEP^*) F(K, L) - WL$$

K and m are assumed to be fixed. Profit maximization by producers then results in equating the net marginal revenue product of labour to the nominal wage rate. That is

$$(P - mEP^*)F_L = W$$

or $\quad F_L = \dfrac{W}{P - mEP^*} = \dfrac{W/P}{1 - m/T}$

the inverse of which gives the labour demand function

$$L^d = L^d \left(\frac{W}{P - mEP^*} \right) = L^d \left(\frac{W/P}{1 - m/T} \right), L^{d'} < 0$$

Thus labour demand is inversely proportional to the product wage, which in turn is a function of the real wage (W/P) and the terms of trade (T). This is shown in Figure 3.8 as the downward sloping labour demand curve on the real-wage-employment plane. Its position depends on the value of T. At a constant real wage rate, an improvement

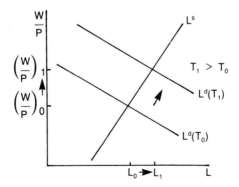

Figure 3.8 The terms of trade and labour market equilibrium
Source: NRI.

61

(deterioration) in the terms of trade implies a lower (higher) product wage so that the demand for labour increases (decreases) and the labour demand curve shifts to the right (left).

Labour supply is assumed to be an increasing function of the real wage rate. That is,

$$L^s = L^s(W/P), \quad L^{s\prime} > 0$$

This is depicted in Figure 3.8 as the upward-sloping labour supply curve.

Equilibrium in the labour market requires that

$$L^d = L^s$$

which also defines the equilibrium level of employment L. That is

$$L = L^s$$

The last four equations form a system that can be solved for L^s, L^d, L and W/P in terms of T. Specifically, we have

$$L^s = L^d = L = L(T), \quad L' > 0$$

and $W/P = W(T), \quad W' > 0$

From the production functions, we also have

$$Y = Y(T), \quad Y' > 0$$

which summarizes the supply side of the economy. The magnitude of the responsiveness of output to changes in the terms of trade (as measured by Y'), depends (among other things) on the value of m (=M/Q), which measures the degree of openness of the economy.

Thus the terms of trade play a crucial role in determining aggregate supply. Once the terms of trade is known, output and employment, as well as the real wage and the product wage, are uniquely determined. Given the capital stock, the labour supply function and technology, fluctuations in output and employment must then be the result of disturbances that alter the terms of trade.

4

AN OPTIMAL PEG FOR THE ASIAN CURRENCIES

INTRODUCTION[1]

The Asian countries have, up to now, focused on the bilateral rates between their local currencies and the dollar when formulating exchange-rate policy, in view of their traditional dependence on the US economy. However, they have experienced drastic changes in their regional composition of trade and inflows of foreign direct investment, and wide fluctuations in economic growth brought about by the global exchange-rate realignment since 1985. Indeed, the yen–dollar rate has replaced the US economic growth rate as the major determinant of short-term economic growth in the Asian NIEs as we have seen in Chapter 3. To adapt to the new international environment, the traditional exchange-rate policy of pegging loosely to the dollar may have to be amended, and more emphasis may have to be put on other major currencies, the Japanese yen in particular.

In this chapter, the literature on optimal currency pegs for developing countries is applied to examine the implications for the economic stability of the Asian countries when they choose to peg their currencies to the yen instead of other (baskets of) currencies. Special attention is paid to the objective of stabilizing output in the face of fluctuating exchange rates among major currencies. At the same time, the role played by economic structures – trade relations with Japan in particular – is also emphasized. To provide a background, we start by summarizing the exchange-rate regimes of the Asian countries. We then move on to formulate a model that shows the relations between exchange-rate fluctuations and short-term economic growth for a small open economy and test it with Korean data. Based on this model, we study the role of exchange-rate policy in output stabilization and derive for an Asian country the optimal peg that minimizes output fluctuations.

EXCHANGE-RATE REGIMES OF THE ASIAN COUNTRIES

The Asian countries have maintained relatively more stable exchange rates against the US dollar than against other currencies (Figure 4.1). In all the Asian NIEs (South Korea, Taiwan, Hong Kong and Singapore) and ASEAN countries (Indonesia, Malaysia, Philippines and Thailand), local currencies have in general shown higher volatility against the yen and the SDR, as measured by the standard deviations of the month-on-month percentage changes since 1973. Exceptions are the Singapore dollar and the Malaysian ringgit, which have exhibited higher volatility against the dollar than against the SDR.

Consistent with global trends, most of the exchange-rate regimes of the Asian countries have gradually shifted from pegging to a single currency (predominantly the dollar) to more flexible arrangements since the breakdown of the Bretton Woods system in the early 1970s. According to the notification of exchange arrangements that member countries furnish to the International Monetary Fund (IMF, 1992), Malaysia and Thailand currently peg their currencies to currency baskets; Hong Kong[2], Indonesia, South Korea and Singapore have exchange-rate regimes characterized by managed floating; and the Philippines allows its currency to float independently. Taiwan does not notify the IMF about its exchange arrangements (as it is not a member), but if it did, the New Taiwan dollar would probably be classified as independently floating. Back in 1974, the majority of the Asian currencies (Korean won, New Taiwan dollar, Hong Kong dollar, Indonesian rupiah and Thai baht) were pegged to the dollar, and only Malaysia, Singapore and the Philippines did not maintain exchange rates within relatively narrow margins against the US currency.

Despite the trend towards more flexible exchange rates against the dollar, the volatility of the Asian currencies against the yen has not diminished in recent years. This casts doubt over the claim that, reflecting the yen's growing importance in exchange-rate policies in Asia, Tokyo has recently acquired a dominant influence over interest rates in some Asian countries (Frankel, 1991a).[3]

EXCHANGE-RATE FLUCTUATIONS AND SHORT-TERM ECONOMIC GROWTH

In this section we examine the relations between exchange rate changes and output fluctuations with a simple economic model. In addition to the exchange rate against the dollar, the yen–dollar rate (and oil prices) will be emphasized. Specific attention will be paid to Japan's dual role as the major competitor and supplier of imports for the Asian countries. Our model is then tested using Korean data.

Theoretical analysis

The model that follows is an extension of the one used in Chapter 3, taking into account the impact of changes in the exchange rate of the domestic currency on output. (A mathematical formulation of this model can be found in Appendix 1 at the end of this chapter). Here, the nominal wage rate is taken to be sticky in the short run (the Keynesian assumption) instead of moving flexibly to clear the labour market (the classical assumption). In addition to the terms of trade, changes in the real wage rate resulting from movements in export prices provide an additional channel through which fluctuations in the exchange rates of third currencies affect national output. Output stabilization can be achieved by manipulating the exchange rate of the domestic currency, which affects output through its impact on the real wage rate.

As we have seen in Chapter 3, economic growth in the Asian NIEs tends to rise as the yen appreciates and decline as the yen depreciates, reflecting the fact that Japan is more a competitor than a supplier of imports for them. A stronger yen, for example, tends to raise their export prices more than import prices. The resulting improvement in their terms of trade boosts output. Given the nominal wage rate, this output-expansion effect is reinforced by the decline in the real wage rate accompanying the increase in export prices.

In contrast, an appreciation of the yen tends to depress the ASEAN countries' terms of trade, reflecting the fact that Japan is more a supplier than a competitor for them. Assuming that the nominal wage rate is rigid in the short run, an increase in export prices (output prices) resulting from the yen's appreciation also boosts output by reducing the real wage rate. This effect is expected to be smaller for the ASEAN countries than for the Asian NIEs, whose export prices are more sensitive to changes in the yen–dollar rate.

Put together, an appreciation of the yen tends to raise output in the Asian NIEs by improving their terms of trade and reducing their real wage rates. In contrast, it tends to reduce output in the ASEAN countries, as the negative effect on output of a deterioration in the terms of trade is likely to more than offset the positive effect of a decline in real wage rates.

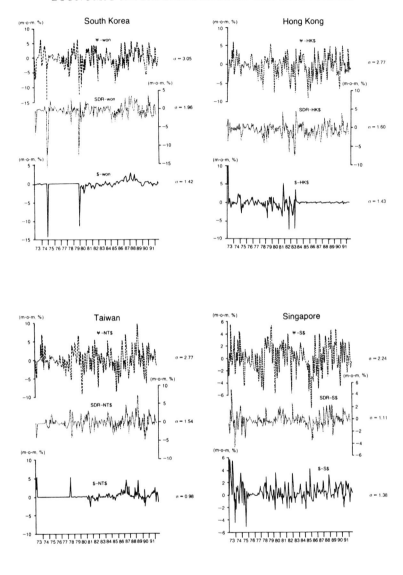

Figure 4.1 Volatility of the Asian currencies

Note: σ denotes standard deviation of m-o-m changes.

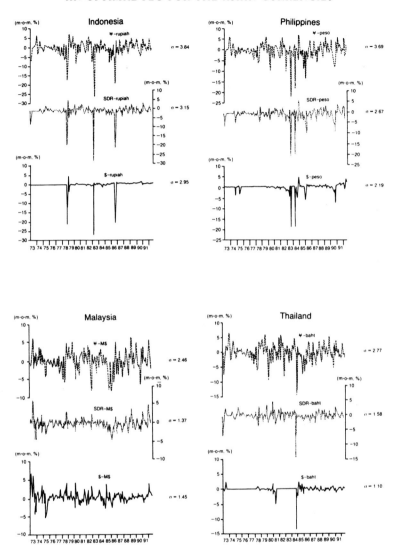

Figure 4.1 cont.

Source: Compiled by NRI based on IMF, *International Financial Statistics* and official statistics of Hong Kong and Taiwan.

67

In addition to the yen–dollar rate, oil prices are a major determinant of short-term output fluctuations in the Asian countries. An increase in oil prices, which is analogous to an appreciation of the currency of OPEC, boosts output in the oil-exporting countries by improving their terms of trade (and depressing their real wage rates), and depresses output in the oil-importing countries through reducing their terms of trade.

The exchange rate of the domestic currency against the dollar can be considered a policy variable at the government's disposal. Changes in the exchange rate of the domestic currency against the dollar affect output through their impact on the real wage rate. Given the nominal wage rate, a devaluation of the local currency raises output prices in local currency terms and reduces the real wage rate, which in turn boosts output. In contrast to changes in foreign exchange rates (such as the yen–dollar rate), the impact of changes in the exchange rate of the domestic currency on output through the terms of trade is negligible in the Asian countries, because they are too small to have price-setting power in international markets.

Empirical evidence

Our model can now be tested using data from South Korea. For simplicity, among the foreign exchange rates, we limit ourselves to the yen–dollar rate and oil prices, which have the largest impact on the Korean economy. The results, as summarized in Table 4.1, support our formulation of the relations between exchange rate and output fluctuations in the Korean economy. The following points are worth noting.

First, Korean output (as measured by industrial production) tends to be more sensitive to changes in the terms of trade than changes in the real wage rate, rising by 1.071 per cent with a 1.0 per cent improvement in the terms of trade and only 0.399 per cent with a 1.0 per cent decrease in the real wage rate.

Second, an appreciation of the yen against the dollar tends to raise both Korean export prices and import prices, with the impact on the former being larger than on the latter. A 1.0 per cent appreciation of the yen raises export prices by 0.394 per cent and import prices by 0.261 per cent, boosting the terms of trade by 0.133 per cent. This reflects the fact that Japan is more a competitor of, than a supplier for, Korea.

Third, an increase in oil prices tends to raise Korean import prices more than export prices, so that the terms of trade deteriorate as a result. This reflects the fact that South Korea is a net importer of oil.

Table 4.1 Estimation of Korean output and trade prices

Dependent variables	Time	Oil prices	¥–$ rate	Terms of trade	Real wage rate	$\bar{R}^2$	D.W.
			Independent variables				
Industrial production	0.029 (52.47)	–	–	–	–	0.985	0.390
Industrial production	0.030 (20.68)	–	–	1.071 (5.25)	−0.399 (−5.10)	0.989	0.761
Industrial production	0.025 (34.48)	−0.141 (−2.81)	−0.220 (−6.28)	–	–	0.993	1.064
Export prices	0.003 (3.88)	0.322 (6.07)	−0.394 (−10.54)	–	–	0.936	0.730
Import prices	−0.002 (−2.92)	0.416 (7.16)	−0.261 (−6.43)	–	–	0.754	0.945
Terms of trade	0.005 (8.03)	−0.094 (−2.01)	−0.133 (−4.07)	–	–	0.926	1.377

Notes: 1 Sample period: 1980Q1–1990Q4, figures for industrial production are seasonally adjusted. 2 Figures in ( ) denote t-values. 3 Except for time trend, all variables are in log form so that the coefficients correspond to elasticities. 4 Shiller lags of appropriate length used in estimation and figures show cumulative effect.
Source: NRI.

OUTPUT STABILIZATION AND THE OPTIMAL PEG

In this section we examine the role of exchange-rate policy in output stabilization and derive the optimal peg for an Asian country seeking to minimize output fluctuations that result from changes in exchange rates and oil prices.

A brief survey of literature

The literature on optimal pegs for developing countries (or small open economies) attempts to evaluate the costs and benefits of pegging to some currency or basket of currencies (or participation in a monetary union) from the viewpoint of the self-interest of the particular region or country. A number of criteria have been considered relevant when a developing country decides to which currency or basket of currencies it wishes to peg its local currency.[4] As summarized in Table 4.2, choosing a peg usually aims at minimizing the volatility in one or more of the major macroeconomic variables – output, current account, inflation, for example – imposed by movements between third currencies. Different rules have been recommended, but usually they involve pegging to a basket of currencies, whose weights depend on the policy objective(s) as well as the economic structure of the country under consideration.[5] Black (1976), for example, suggests pegging the local currency to a basket weighted to reflect the direction of trade in goods and services in order to stabilize the relative price between tradable and non-tradable goods. Branson and Katseli-Papaefstratiou (1980), however, argue in favor of pegging to a basket weighted to reflect market power in export and import markets so as to stabilize the terms of trade (and thus real income).

The role of exchange-rate policy in output stabilization

Asian governments can offset changes in output resulting from fluctuations in third currencies such as the yen–dollar rate and oil prices (the exchange rate of OPEC) by manipulating the exchange rates of their local currencies. This can be illustrated by considering an appreciation of the yen. In the Asian NIEs, an increase in output resulting from a stronger yen can be offset by revaluing the local currency, which reduces output through raising the real wage rate. In contrast, in the ASEAN countries, a decrease in output resulting from an appreciation of the yen can be offset by devaluing the local currency.

The direction and magnitude of the exchange-rate adjustment needed to achieve output stability in the face of a changing yen–dollar

Table 4.2 Recommended pegs suggested in the literature

Author(s)	Suggested aim	Recommended peg
Black (1976)	Minimize variance of relative price of traded goods	Basket with weights based on direction of total trade in goods and services (or elasticity weights for country with market power), provided the benefits of pegging to a basket outweigh the costs of inability to intervene in the unit providing the peg

Author(s)	Suggested aim	Recommended peg
Crokett & Nsouli (1977)	Stabilize balance of trade and output, by stabilizing EER	Peg to import-weighted basket, with consideration as to whether the SDR is a good proxy
Flanders & Helpman (1979)	a) Minimize variance of the balance of trade subject to a requirement on its expected level, by stabilizing the EER with MERM-type weights	Peg to an elasticity-weighted basket. (Special case with price-inelastic imports and perfectly elastic export demand: export-weighted basket)
	b) Minimize variance of real income subject to a requirement on its expected level	Peg to a basket with large weights for competitors and small or even negative weights for suppliers
Lipschitz (1979)	Minimize variations in resource allocation and income distribution, by stabilizing REER	Peg to a basket, with weights based on currency of denomination of total trade when the export and import-competing sectors are of similar size
Bacha (1981)	Stabilize REER	Consider pegging to a basket
Lipschitz & Sundararajan (1980)	Stabilize REER	Peg to elasticity-weighted basket modified by covariance between inflation and depreciation. (Special case with PPP among trading partners: peg to single currency with preferred inflation rate)
Branson and Katseli-Papaefstratiou (1980)	Stabilize the terms of trade	Peg to basket with weights reflecting market power in export and import markets
Connolly (1982)	Minimize the level and variability of inflation	Peg to the US dollar, or perhaps to the SDR or a trade-weighted basket

Source: Williamson (1982).

rate depends on the following four parameters: (1) the responsiveness (elasticity) of output to changes in the terms of trade (a); (2) the responsiveness (elasticity) of output to changes in the real wage rate (b); (3) the responsiveness (elasticity) of export prices to changes in the yen–dollar rate (α); and (4) the responsiveness (elasticity) of import prices to changes in the yen-dollar rate (β).

These four parameters summarize the economic structures of the host country relevant to the formulation of exchange-rate policy. The value of α reflects more the degree of competitiveness between the exports of the host country and Japan than Japan's share of the host country's exports, as will be emphasized later in this chapter. On the other hand, the value of β comes closer to Japan's share of the host country's imports. This asymmetry reflects the fact that international prices are largely determined by the exchange rates of the exporting countries rather than those of the importing countries, since countries usually have more monopoly power on the export side than on the import side in international trade.

The impact of fluctuations in oil prices on output can also be offset by manipulating the exchange rate of the local currency. As seen above, an increase in oil prices boosts output in the oil-exporting countries but reduces that in oil-importing countries through its impact on the terms of trade. To stabilize output, an oil-importing country should devalue its local currency to stimulate production as oil prices increase, while an oil-exporting country should revalue its local currency to suppress production. The direction and magnitude of the exchange-rate adjustment needed to achieve output stability in the face of changing oil prices will again depend on the four parameters just cited, with α and β interpreted, respectively, as the responsiveness of export and imports prices in the host country to changes in oil prices.

Choosing the optimal peg

Pegging to a basket of currencies provides an automatic way for the Asian countries to stabilize output fluctuations arising from changes in third country exchange rates, such as the yen–dollar rate. In a multi-currency framework, the weight of a foreign currency in the 'optimal basket' can be derived as follows. (For a mathematical formulation, see Appendix 2 at the end of this chapter).

The weight θ_i of currency i in the optimal basket that stabilizes output depends on (1) the elasticity of output with respect to currency i's exchange rate (against the dollar) and (2) the elasticity of output with respect to the domestic exchange rate. In what follows, currency i refers to the yen, so that θ_i denotes the weight of the yen in the optimal basket for the host country.

The elasticity of output with respect to the yen–dollar rate in turn can be calculated as the the the sum of: (1) the product of the elasticity of the terms of trade with respect to the yen–dollar rate $(\alpha_i - \beta_i)$ and the elasticity of output with respect to the terms of trade a; and (2) the product of the elasticity of export prices (and thus the real wage rate) with respect to the yen–dollar rate α_i and the elasticity of output with respect to the real wage rate b.

On the other hand, the elasticity of output with respect to the domestic exchange rate is equal to the elasticity of output with respect to the real wage rate b.

The optimal weight of currency i (the yen in the present case) in the currency basket is given by the elasticity of output with respect to currency i's exchange rate $a(\alpha_i - \beta_i) + b\alpha_i$ divided by the elasticity of output with respect to the domestic exchange rate b. That is

$$\theta_i = \frac{a(\alpha_i - \beta_i) + b\alpha_i}{b}$$

A country whose terms of trade benefit from an appreciation of the yen (with $\alpha_i - \beta_i > 0$), as in the case of South Korea, should include a substantial weight for the yen in its basket. In extreme cases, the yen may have a weight larger than 100 per cent.

On the other hand, in a developing country that depends on Japan heavily for imports but does not compete with it directly (with $\alpha_i - \beta_i < 0$), as in the case of Malaysia, the optimal basket may involve a negative weight for the yen. An appreciation of the yen reduces output (as the negative effect on output of the resulting deterioration in the terms of trade is not compensated for by the positive effect acting through the resulting decline in the real wage rate), and thus requires a depreciation of the domestic currency to restore output (through reducing the real wage rate).

When country i refers to OPEC, the above equation suggests that an oil-importing country should assign a negative weight to oil prices when considering pegging to a basket of currencies. In contrast, in oil-exporting countries, pegging to a basket of currencies that involves a large positive weight for oil prices may help stabilize output.

The Korean case can be used to illustrate how pegging to a basket can help stabilize output (Figure 4.2). Using the parameters estimated above, the optimal peg for the Korean won would be composed of: yen

Change in South Korean output (%)

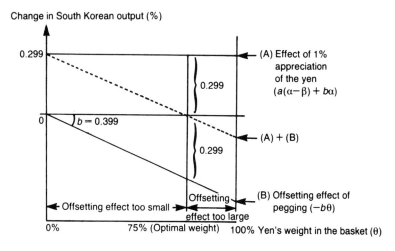

Figure 4.2 Output-stabilization effect of pegging to a basket of currencies
Source: NRI.

75 per cent ($\alpha = 0.394$, $\beta = 0.261$, $a = 1.071$, $b = 0.399$), oil -8 per cent ($\alpha = 0.322$, $\beta = 0.416$, $a = 1.071$, $b = 0.399$), and dollar 33 per cent ($100 - 75 + 8$). When the yen appreciates by 1.0 per cent against the dollar, for example, Korea's export and import prices rise by 0.394 per cent and 0.261 per cent, respectively, so that the terms of trade improve by 0.133 per cent. At the same time, given the nominal wage rate and the won rate against the dollar, the real wage rate drops by 0.394 per cent. As a result, output rises by 0.299 per cent ($0.133\% \times 1.071 = 0.142\%$ through an improvement in the terms of trade, plus $0.394\% \times 0.399 = 0.157\%$ through a decline in the real wage rate). To reduce output by the same amount requires raising the real wage rate by 0.75 per cent ($0.299\%/0.399$) which can be brought about by revaluing the won against the dollar by 0.75 per cent. This can be achieved automatically when the won is pegged to a basket of currencies in which the yen carries a weight of 75 per cent (the optimal weight for the yen calculated above). Likewise, when the yen depreciates against the dollar by 1.0 per cent, the negative impact on Korean output can be offset by devaluing the won by 0.75 per cent. Again, this can be achieved automatically by pegging the won to a basket of currencies in which the yen carries a weight of 75 per cent.

When the won is pegged to this 'optimal basket' of currencies, a 10 per cent appreciation of the yen against the dollar, for example, would automatically lead to a 7.5 per cent appreciation of the won against the dollar; the positive effect of the 10 per cent appreciation of the yen on Korean output would then be just offset by the negative effect of the 7.5 per cent appreciation of the won. Assigning any other weight to the yen in the basket would imply a counterbalancing force either too small (when the weight is less than 75 per cent) or too large (when the weight is more than 75 per cent) to offset the initial effect.

Concluding remarks

The conclusion can be summarized as follows. For the Asian NIEs, which compete with Japan in international markets, pegging to the yen would promote economic stability. For the ASEAN countries, which have trade structures complementary to, instead of competitive with, that of Japan, however, pegging to the dollar is more compatible with economic stability than pegging to the yen.

So far we have concentrated on the policy objective of stabilizing output, but in reality other macroeconomic objectives need to be taken into consideration when deciding which policy mix to adopt. If the objective is to stabilize domestic prices, for example, the optimal peg would involve assigning a (positive) weight equal to α_i to currency i. For an oil importer, this would magnify the decline (increase) in output as oil prices increase (decrease). Since these objectives may contradict one another, the final choice involves striking an optimal trade-off between them.

For simplicity we have focused on a very narrow aspect of a very broad issue. Our analysis can be expanded to take into consideration the following factors:

1 the determination of the optimal peg under policy objective(s) other than output stability;
2 the role of real and monetary shocks in determining the optimal basket;
3 the role of market power of the host country (by relaxing the small-country assumption);
4 interdependence between Japan and the United States.

The analysis of optimal pegs for the Asian currencies in this chapter provides the starting point for our study of the possibility of forming a yen bloc from an Asian perspective in Chapter 9.

APPENDIX 1: A SIMPLE MODEL OF A SMALL OPEN ECONOMY

The impact of exchange rate changes on the Asian economies can be analysed using the following model (Figure 4.3).

Consider a small open economy that produces a final good Q with the input of domestically owned capital K and labour L, and an imported intermediate good M. We assume that the host country is completely specialized in the production and consumption of Q, so that Q is also the only (composite) good exported. For simplicity, we also assume that M is the only (composite) good imported. Output (net of imports) Y is given by Q−M.

Let W denote the nominal wage rate in the local currency, E the exchange rate of the domestic currency against the dollar (the numeraire against which the exchange rates of all currencies are expressed), and P_x and P_m the nominal price of the final product (export prices) and the intermediate input (import prices) in terms of the dollar. By the small-country assumption, P_x and P_m are unaffected by developments in the domestic economy, and the price elasticity of the host country's aggregate demand is infinitely large. This allows us to focus on the supply side of the economy. The price of the final product in terms of domestic currency units is given by EP_x and that of the intermediate input by EP_m. The terms of trade and the real wage rate are given by P_x/P_m and W/EP_x, respectively.

Profit maximization implies that[6]

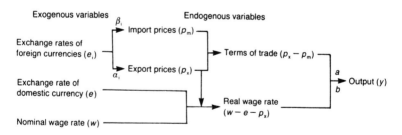

Figure 4.3 Model for impact of exchange-rate fluctuations on economic growth

Notes: All variables are expressed in natural log form. All exchange rates are measured in terms of domestic currencies per US dollar. Import and export prices are measured in terms of the US dollar, and the nominal wage rate is measured in terms of the domestic currency. The parameters a and b measure the elasticity of output with respect to the terms of trade and to the real wage rate, respectively, while α_i and β_i measure the elasticity of export prices and import prices with respect to the exchange rate of foreign currency i.

Source: NRI.

$$y = a(p_x - p_m) - b(w - e - p_x) \tag{1}$$

where small letters denote the natural log value of the corresponding variables in capital letters and

a = elasticity of output with respect to the terms of trade
b = elasticity of output with respect to the real wage rate

with $a > 0$ and $b > 0$. The values of a and b depend on the shares of K, L, M in production and their substitutability for each other.

Equation (1) shows that output rises with an improvement in the terms of trade $p_x - p_m$ and falls with an increase in the real wage rate $w - e - p_x$ (a decline in competitiveness), with the responsiveness denoted by a and b, respectively.

To examine the impact of exchange rate changes on output, factors determining p_x and p_m needed to be specified. Here (changes in) import and export prices (in terms of the US dollar, the numeraire) are taken as a function of export prices of foreign countries (country 1, 2, ... n), which in turn depend on (changes in) the exchange rates of their currencies against the dollar (e_i). The exchange rate of the domestic currency against the dollar can be excluded by the small-country assumption. That is

$$p_x = -\sum_{i=1}^{n} \alpha_i e_i \tag{2}$$

$$p_m = -\sum_{i=1}^{n} \beta_i e_i \tag{3}$$

with $\alpha_i > 0$ and $\beta_i > 0$ for all i. The terms of trade is given by

$$t = -\sum_{i=1}^{n} (\alpha_i - \beta_i) e_i$$

The exchange rate of the dollar (against itself) is 1.0 in absolute terms and zero in log form (that is, when the United States is taken as country n, $e_n = 0$). In our model all exchange rates are taken to be exogenous variables. By the small-country assumption, $\sum \alpha_i = 1$ and $\sum \beta_i = 1$ (where i includes the United States).

The parameters α_i and β_i summarize the trade structures of the host country. The value of α_i measures the responsiveness of the host country's export prices to changes in the exchange rate of country i's currency against the dollar. It reflects more the degree of competitiveness between the exports of the host country and country i than country

i's share of the host country's exports. On the other hand, the value of β_i, which measures the responsiveness of import prices to changes in the exchange rate of county i's currency against the dollar, comes closer to country i's share of the host country's imports.

When $\alpha_i > \beta_i$, an appreciation of country i's currency against the dollar raises the host country's terms of trade. This occurs when country i is more a competitor (and/or a market) of, than a supplier for, the host country, as in the case when the host country is Korea and country i is Japan. On the other hand, when $\alpha_i < \beta_i$, an appreciation of currency i lowers the terms of trade, as in the case when the host country is Malaysia and country i is Japan (see Chapter 3).

When p_x and p_m also depend on oil prices (acting directly or indirectly through import and export prices of third countries), oil can be treated formally as a currency (the currency of OPEC, for example), with its exchange rate against the dollar given by the reciprocal of oil prices measured in dollar terms. We follow this convention in the rest of the text.

Substituting equations (2) and (3) into equation (1) and rearranging gives

$$y = -\sum_{i=1}^{n} e_i[a(\alpha_i - \beta_i) + b a_i] + be - bw \tag{4}$$

Equation (4) shows that an appreciation of currency i can raise or reduce output, depending on the relative magnitude of a, b, α_i and β_i. In the case when $\alpha_i > \beta_i$, an appreciation of currency i raises output through both the terms-of-trade effect and the competitive effect. In the case when $\alpha_t < \beta_i$, the terms-of-trade effect and the competitive effect tend to offset one another; when α_i is small, an appreciation of currency i can reduce the output of the host country.

The exchange rate of the domestic currency against the dollar is considered a policy variable at the government's disposal, while the nominal wage rate is considered exogenous (Keynesian wage rigidity). A depreciation of the domestic currency against the dollar boosts output through reducing the real wage rate, although by the small-country assumption it does not act through the terms of trade. A decrease in the nominal wage rate has a similar effect.

APPENDIX 2: DERIVATION OF THE OPTIMAL PEG TO STABILIZE OUTPUT

Based on the analysis in Appendix 1, we now compare the volatility of output under alternative pegging schemes and derive the optimal peg for an Asian country that seeks to minimize output fluctuations resulting from exchange rate changes.

Equation (4) furnishes the starting point of our analysis of output volatility under alternative pegging schemes – pegging to the dollar and pegging to the yen.[7] For simplicity, changes in oil prices and the nominal wage rate are neglected, and the yen and the dollar are taken as the only two foreign currencies. Equation (4) can be simplified to

$$y = -e_J[a(\alpha_J - \beta_J) + ba_J] + be \qquad (4a)$$

where e_J denotes the yen–dollar rate, and α_J and β_J denote the yen–dollar rate elasticities of export prices and import prices respectively.

First consider the case of pegging to the yen, that is $e = e_J$. Equation (4a) can then be simplified to

$$y = -e_J[a(\alpha_J - \beta_J) + ba_J - b]$$

The volatility of y in terms of its variance is given by[8]

$$\text{Var}(y) = \{-[a(\alpha_J - \beta_J) + ba_J - b]\}^2 \text{Var}(e_J) \qquad (5)$$

When the domestic currency is pegged to the dollar, that is $e = 0$, equation (4a) becomes

$$y = -e_J[a(\alpha_J - \beta_J) + ba_J]$$

and

$$\text{Var}(y) = \{-[a(\alpha_J - \beta_J) + ba_J]^2\}\text{Var}(e_J) \qquad (6)$$

For a given $\text{Var}(e_J)$, pegging to the yen would imply a smaller $\text{Var}(y)$ when

$$|a(\alpha_J - \beta_J) + ba_J - b| < |a(\alpha_J - \beta_J) + ba_J|$$

The Asian NIEs, which are competitors of Japan (with large α_J) are likely to meet this condition. On the other hand, for the ASEAN countries, which do not compete much with Japan but depend heavily on it for imports (with small α_J but large β_J), pegging to the dollar may be more commensurate with output stability.

Pegging to a basket of currencies (or an effective exchange rate) provides one way of stabilizing the economy. As seen above, an appreciation of currency i against the dollar can raise or lower output of the host country, depending on the relative values of α_i and β_i. On the other hand, an appreciation (depreciation) of the domestic currency lowers (raises) output by raising (lowering) the real wage rate. Output fluctuations resulting from changes in foreign exchange rates (and oil prices) can be offset by manipulating the exchange rate of the domestic currency. Pegging to a basket of currencies provides an automatic way in which this can be achieved.

The choice of an optimal basket depends on the policy objective(s) of the host country, but here we limit ourselves to that of minimizing fluctuations in output resulting from movements in foreign exchange rates (including oil prices). When the host country chooses to peg its currency to a basket of currencies by assigning a fixed weight of θ_i in the basket to currency i, the exchange rate of the local currency against the dollar is given by the weighted average of the exchange rates of all other currencies against the dollar, with the weights given by θ_i. That is

$$e = -\sum_{i=1}^{n} \theta_i e_i \tag{7}$$

Substituting equation (7) into equation (4) and ignoring changes in the nominal wage rate (which is exogenously determined) gives

$$y = -\sum_{i=1}^{n} e_i[a(\alpha_i - \beta_i) + ba_i] + b\sum_{i=1}^{n} \theta_i e_i \tag{8}$$

Assuming that foreign exchange rates are not correlated with one another, minimizing the variance of y can be achieved by setting $y = 0$ in equation (8). This condition is met when the weight for each foreign currency θ_i is set so that

$$\theta_i = \frac{a(\alpha_i - \beta_i) + ba_i}{b} \tag{9}$$

which gives the optimal weight for currency i. Equation (9) shows that the weight assigned to one currency in the optimal peg may differ from one host country to another, reflecting the differences in their economic structures (as summarized by a, b, α_i and β_i).

A number of special cases are worth noting. When the imported good is a final good for consumption instead of an intermediate good for production, $a = 0$ and output is independent of the terms of trade. In this case, the optimal weight for country i reduces to α_i. Furthermore, if α_i reflects export share instead of the degree of competitiveness, the weight in the optimal peg for country i then corresponds to its share of the host country's exports.

5

THE FLYING-GEESE PATTERN OF CHANGING TRADE STRUCTURE

INTRODUCTION[1]

The commodity composition of trade in the Asia-Pacific region countries is undergoing drastic changes. Manufactured exports from Asia's developing countries have grown in importance and the traditional pattern of intra-regional trade, dominated by the exchange of manufactured and primary commodities between Japan and the developing countries, is giving way to one characterized by trade in manufactured goods (intra-industry trade) among countries at different stages of economic development. This chapter first describes the evolution of the Asian countries' commodity composition of trade in the course of economic development by using the 'flying-geese model'.[2] This is then followed by a closer look at the recent trends in rising intra-industry trade, which has been made possible by the progress in industrialization in the developing countries of the region.

THE CHANGING COMMODITY COMPOSITION OF TRADE

The flying-geese model of changing comparative advantage

The flying-geese model was first used to describe the life cycles of industries in the course of economic development (Akamatsu, 1962). In its original form, the focus is on specific industries in specific countries. The flying-geese model has been extended to study the dynamic changes in the industrial structure (that is, the rise and fall of different industries) in specific countries, and further to the shift of industries from one country to another (Yamazawa, 1990a).

In the original form of the flying-geese model, the life cycle of a particular industry is represented by the trends in the value (or volume) of imports, production and exports. For a particular industry, the level of imports first rises and then declines. The same rise-and-fall pattern is later repeated by domestic production and by exports. When plotted against time, imports, domestic production and exports form a pattern of overlapping inverted V-shaped curves like wild geese flying in orderly ranks. The analysis can be simplified by referring to an indicator of comparative advantage. For example, the evolution of the ratio between production and consumption (or domestic demand) over the life cycle for an industry also takes the form of an inverted V-shaped curve (Figure 5.1).[3]

In general, each industry passes through five stages – introduction stage, import-substitution stage, export stage, mature stage, and reverse-import stage. In the introduction stage domestic production

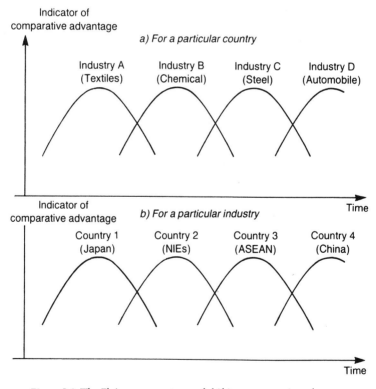

Figure 5.1 The Flying-geese pattern of shifting comparative advantage
Source: Based on Yamazawa (1990b) with adaptations.

starts through imitation or transfer of technology, but the domestic market remains dominated by imports. In the import-substitution stage domestic production expands at a faster pace than demand so that imports start to fall. The industry moves to the export stage when production expands to surpass domestic demand so that there is a surplus for exports. In the mature stage, production and exports start to decline on the back of rising production costs, and investment in less developed countries accelerates. Finally, the reverse-import stage is reached when the industry becomes a net importer again, with part of the imports coming from overseas subsidiaries of the country concerned.

Capital accumulation (including the inflow of foreign direct investment) and forward and backward linkages with other industries, by changing the comparative advantage of the country concerned, usually leads to an upgrading of industrial structure. This can be represented by repeating the inverted V-shaped curve showing the production/consumption ratio for emerging industries which are usually more capital- and technology-intensive than the preceding ones (Figure 5.1a). A typical sequence seen among Asian countries is the shift from the textiles industry to the chemical industry and than further to the steel industry and the automobile industry.

When extended to the context of an open economy, the flying-geese model is used to describe the shifting of industries from more advanced countries to countries catching up from behind. This is shown in Figure 5.1b, with the inverted V-shaped curves now representing the same industry in different countries (instead of different industries in the same country). A typical example is the shifting of textile production from Japan to the Asian NIEs and then further to the ASEAN countries and China.

The flying-geese model explains shifting competitiveness of an industry over time by focusing on the dynamic *changes in factor endowment* of countries in the course of economic development. In addition to the indigenous improvement in the availability and quality of factor endowments in the countries catching up from behind, foreign direct investment, by transferring factors of production (capital, technology and management know-how, for example) from the more advanced countries to the less developed ones, also helps promote the evolution of trade structure. The flying-geese model should be distinguished from the product cycle theory (Vernon, 1966) which emphasizes the *changes in the production process* (particularly the combination of factors of production) over time, taking factor endowment in the countries involved as given. Both the flying-geese and the product cycle models emphasize the role of foreign direct investment. While the flying-geese model focuses on the receiving country, the product cycle model concentrates on the behaviour of the investing country.

Four stages of trade structure

The flying-geese pattern can now be applied to examine the changes in the Asian countries' commodity composition of trade. In the course of economic development, a country's comparative advantage usually shifts from the production of primary commodities to labour-intensive manufactured goods and later on, to capital- and technology-intensive products. This shift is reflected in the trade structure as it evolves from that of a developing country to that of a newly industrializing country and finally to one typical of an industrialized country.

Instead of following the traditional approach of looking at the trends in production, imports and exports, we can show the changes in (revealed) comparative advantage of a country's various industries by calculating the respective specialization indexes of the industries.[4] For a certain industry, say industry k, the specialization index is defined by the following equation

Specialization Index of industry k

$$= \frac{\text{Exports} - \text{Imports in industry k}}{\text{Exports} + \text{Imports in industry k}}$$

Thus, the specialization index is simply the trade balance standardized by the volume of two-way trade for the industry under consideration. From this definition, the values can range from -1 to $+1$, with a higher value implying stronger international competitiveness.

A country's trade structure can be classified into one of four categories according to the relative magnitude of the specialization indexes of primary commodities, machinery and other manufactures.[5] Because a country typically passes from one category to the next in a certain sequence (from developing country to young NIE to mature NIE and finally to industrialized country), we refer to our classification as the four stages of trade structure (Figure 5.2).

A nation at the developing country stage usually has a weak industrial base and must depend on imports not only for capital goods but also for other manufactures. The manufacturing sector as a whole runs a large

a) Definition

		Specialization index			Examples
I.	Developing country stage	Primary commodities	> Other manufactures	> Machinery	Indonesia, Thailand
II.	Young NIE stage	Other manufactures	> Primary commodities	> Machinery	Philippines
III.	Mature NIE stage	Other manufactures	> Machinery	Primary > commodities	Hong Kong, Korea
IV.	Industrialized country stage	Machinery	> Other manufactures	Primary > commodities	Singapore, Japan

b) Changes in the specialization indexes over time

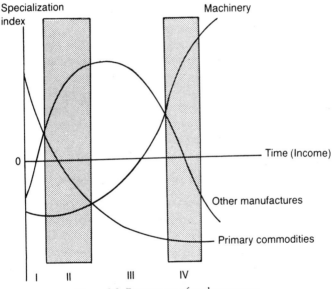

Figure 5.2 Four stages of trade structure
Source: NRI.

deficit that must be financed by earnings from exports of primary commodities. For this pattern of trade, the specialization index is high for primary commodities and low for machinery and other manufactures.

Early in the process of industrialization, progress is made in the import substitution of other manufactures, and the specialization index of other manufactures begins to rise. As that index surpasses the index

85

of primary commodities, the trade structure enters the young NIE stage.

As economic development gathers pace, progress is also made in the import substitution of machinery, and that specialization index begins to rise. At the same time, as labour flows into the industrial sector, the importance of the agricultural sector begins to fall. Shrinking exports of agricultural products and rising imports of raw materials (to support the expanding manufacturing sector) cause the fall of the specialization index of primary commodities to accelerate. When the specialization index of machinery surpasses that of primary products, the trade structure enters the mature NIE stage.

As income continues to rise, an increase in labour costs reduces the export competitiveness of other manufactures, and comparative advantage shifts to capital- and technology-intensive products. Declining industries are relocated overseas to release resources for expanding industries. Thus, the specialization index of machinery surpasses that of other manufactures and the trade structure reaches its final stage, the industrialized country stage.

It goes without saying that trade structure depends not only on the level of economic development but also on the endowment of natural resources. Thus, resource-rich countries such as Australia and the oil-producing countries in the Middle East have trade structures typical of developing countries despite high income levels. The simplified model helps to focus on the relationship between economic development and trade structure in the Asian countries.

Asian countries' stages of trade structure

The trade structures of the Asian countries vary substantially from one another and have changed dramatically over time, reflecting high economic growth and the disparity in regional incomes (Table 5.1 and Table 5.2). To expand on this point, let us examine how Asian countries' trade structures have evolved since the mid-1960s using the stages of trade structure framework described above (Table 5.3).

In 1965, Japan's trade structure was at the mature NIE stage, with other manufactures as the leading export sector. This was broadly in line with Japan's stage of economic development at the time. The subsequent surge in exports of machinery, particularly automobiles, and the decline of labour-intensive industries moved Japan's trade structure into the industrialized country stage.

The trade structure of Taiwan has advanced at a more rapid pace than that of South Korea. Starting from the developing country stage,

Table 5.1 Asian countries' commodity composition of trade (%)

	Exports												Imports											
	Primary commodities				Other manufactures				Machinery				Primary commodities				Other manufactures				Machinery			
	65	75	88	90	65	75	88	90	65	75	88	90	65	75	88	90	65	75	88	90	65	75	88	90
South Korea	40	18	7	7	56	68	54	57	3	14	39	37	48	49	35	36	38	24	30	29	13	26	35	34
Taiwan	58	19	8	4	37	62	58	58	4	20	34	38	43	41	29	18	29	27	35	51	29	32	36	31
Hong Kong	6	3	3	4	87	82	72	73	7	15	25	23	41	41	17	13	46	42	54	60	13	17	30	26
Singapore	65	48	23	27	24	29	24	25	10	22	53	48	55	32	24	26	30	40	31	32	14	27	45	42
Indonesia	96	99	71	64	1	1	28	34	3	0	1	1	11	23	26	23	50	40	36	35	39	37	39	43
Malaysia	94	82	55	56	4	12	19	17	2	6	26	27	47	38	26	22	32	30	28	33	22	33	47	45
Philippines	95	83	38	38	6	17	52	52	0	1	10	10	37	37	30	40	30	31	50	50	33	32	20	20
Thailand	95	82	48	36	4	16	41	44	0	2	11	20	21	34	27	22	49	31	36	37	31	35	37	41
China	54	na	27	26	43	na	69	56	3	na	4	17	61	na	10	19	27	na	49	39	12	na	41	41
Australia	86	81	75	63	10	13	17	30	5	6	8	6	23	20	14	14	41	40	47	44	37	41	39	42
USA	35	31	23	22	28	26	31	31	37	43	47	47	49	46	21	24	36	29	36	36	14	25	43	40
Japan	9	4	2	2	60	47	33	32	31	49	65	66	80	82	58	55	11	11	30	30	9	7	13	16

Source: World Bank, World Development Report, various issues.

Table 5.2 Specialization indexes of the Asian countries

	Primary commodities				Other manufactures				Machinery			
	1965	1975	1988	1990	1965	1975	1988	1990	1965	1975	1988	1990
South Korea	-0.52	-0.59	-0.62	-0.69	-0.28	0.32	0.36	0.29	-0.84	-0.46	0.14	0.01
Taiwan	0.26	-0.42	-0.50	-0.55	0.24	0.34	0.34	0.16	-0.71	-0.29	0.07	0.20
Hong Kong	-0.81	-0.87	-0.69	-0.53	0.31	0.26	0.13	0.10	-0.30	-0.16	-0.09	-0.06
Singapore	-0.03	-0.11	-0.11	-0.05	-0.11	-0.44	-0.20	-0.19	-0.17	-0.39	-0.01	0.00
Indonesia	0.82	0.74	0.60	0.53	-0.96	-0.95	0.06	0.06	-0.84	-0.96	-0.93	-0.95
Malaysia	0.39	0.41	0.46	0.44	-0.75	-0.40	-0.07	-0.32	-0.81	-0.66	-0.17	-0.25
Philippines	0.37	0.12	0.01	-0.23	-0.71	-0.51	-0.08	-0.18	-1.00	-0.98	-0.42	-0.50
Thailand	0.59	0.24	0.27	0.06	-0.87	-0.48	0.06	-0.10	-1.00	-0.94	-0.55	-0.49
China	-0.13	na	0.40	0.23	0.16	na	0.10	0.25	-0.64	na	-0.85	-0.35
Australia	0.54	0.66	0.66	0.61	-0.64	-0.44	-0.51	-0.24	-0.78	-0.71	-0.69	-0.77
USA	-0.05	-0.14	-0.14	-0.20	-0.01	0.00	-0.25	-0.23	0.54	0.31	-0.14	-0.08
Japan	-0.79	-0.91	-0.91	-0.91	0.70	0.59	0.22	0.14	0.56	0.76	0.75	0.67

Source: Compiled by NRI based on World Bank, *World Development Report*, various issues.

Table 5.3 Asian countries' stages of trade structure

	Stage of trade structure			
	Developing country	Young NIE	Mature NIE	Industrialized country
South Korea		□————	Δ ————	O
Taiwan	□————————————————		Δ ————	O
Hong Kong			□ – Δ – O	
Singapore			□————	Δ — O
Thailand	□ —— Δ		———— O	
Malaysia	□ —— Δ	———— O		
Philippines	□ ————	Δ – O		
Indonesia	□ – Δ – O			
China		Δ ————	O	
(Australia)	□ – Δ – O			
Japan			□ ————	Δ – O

Note: □ = 1965; Δ = 1990; O = 2000 (forecast).
Source: NRI.

Taiwan's trade structure reached the young NIE stage in 1967, the mature NIE stage in 1972 and the industrialized country stage in 1991 (Figure 5.3). Korea started from the young NIEs stage and has now reached only the mature NIE stage .

Hong Kong and Singapore took advantage of their geographical locations and led Korea and Taiwan in the process of industrialization in the 1960s. Both countries' trade structures had reached the mature NIE stage by 1965. Subsequently, Hong Kong developed into a major exporter of labour-intensive manufactured goods, while Singapore pursued a development strategy based on promoting capital- and technology-intensive industries. Singapore's trade structure has now reached the industrialized country stage, but Hong Kong has lagged behind in upgrading its trade structure.

The appreciation of the NIEs' currencies since 1986 has prompted the relocation of their labour-intensive industries to the ASEAN countries and helped shift their own comparative advantage to higher-value-added products. Taiwan's trade structure reached the industrialized country stage in 1991, when machinery overtook other

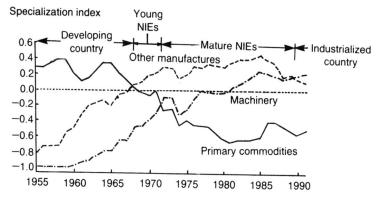

Figure 5.3 Taiwan's stages of trade structure
Source: Compiled by NRI based on Taiwan trade statistics.

manufactures as the leading export sector in terms of the specialization index. South Korea is expected to reach this stage within the next few years. In Hong Kong, the availability of cheap labour across the Chinese border has helped maintain export competitiveness, but it has also delayed the transformation of the trade structure, which will probably remain in the mature NIE stage until the year 2000.

The ASEAN countries still have trade structures typical of developing countries. In recent years, however, the massive inflow of foreign direct investment from Japan and the Asian NIEs has paved the way for radical change. Unlike in the past, recent foreign direct investment has concentrated in the manufacturing sector instead of the resource sector. The ASEAN countries are seizing the chance to reduce their dependence on exports of primary commodities, and industrialization is accelerating. Thailand's trade structure, which is now similar to that of Taiwan in the late-1960s, should reach the young NIE stage in the next few years and the mature NIE stage before 2000 (Figure 5.4). Malaysia and the Philippines, but not oil-dependent Indonesia, will reach the young NIE stage by the turn of the century.

China's trade structure has undergone drastic changes in recent years, thanks to the inflow of direct investment from Hong Kong and Taiwan. By 1990, the specialization index of other manufactures has overtaken that of primary commodities, qualifying China as a young NIE by our classification. Given the current pace of industrialization, China should reach the mature NIE stage before 2000.

Foreign direct investment has played a dominant role in the

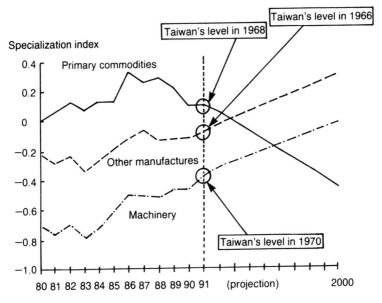

Figure 5.4 Thailand's changing trade structure

Note: Projection based on trends in Taiwan's specialization index since 1966 (for other manufactures), 1968 (for primary commodities) and 1970 (for machinery).

Source: Compiled by NRI based on trade statistics of Thailand and Taiwan.

emergence of new industries and the withering away of old ones. In the case of South Korea, for example, inflows of foreign direct investment laid the foundation for the textile and garment industry in the 1960s. Indeed, the share of textiles and garments in Korea's total exports has been closely related to their share of the cumulative inflow of foreign direct investment. On the other hand, outflows of foreign direct investment helped Japan to reduce the size of its textile industry and release resources for new industries. In a similar evolutionary process, the Asian NIEs are now relocating their labour intensive industries to ASEAN and China.

The stages of trade structure can be verified by showing the relationship between the level of economic development and the specialization indexes (Figure 5.5). For simplicity, per capita GNP (at constant 1990 prices) is used as a proxy for the level of economic development.[6] As expected, the specialization index for primary commodities tends to decline as income rises, while that of machinery tends to increase. The specialization index for other manufactures rises with income over a certain range and then declines.

91

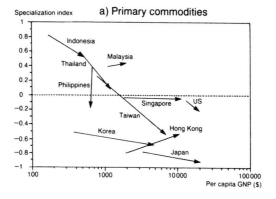

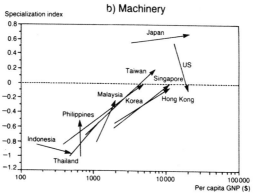

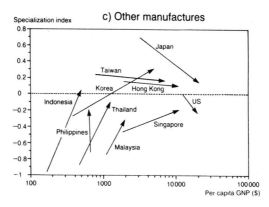

Figure 5.5 Economic development and changes in the specialization indexes
Note: The tails and heads of the arrows indicate the positions in 1965 and 1990
respectively.
Source: NRI.

In a more rigorous analysis, the specialization index for each category is estimated using per capita GNP. The sample is formed by pooling time series (1965 and 1990) and cross-sectional data (Asian NIEs, ASEAN, Japan and the United States). In the case of other manufactures, the square of per capita GNP is included to take into account the backward bending section of the specialization index. The result, as summarized in Table 5.4, supports our contention that the level of economic development is important in determining the commodity composition of trade.

GROWING INTRA-INDUSTRY TRADE

Intra-industry trade refers to the interchange of products belonging to the same industry. Thus, for a particular industry k, the degree of intra-industry trade between two countries (i and j) can be measured as follows

$$\text{Index of intra-industry trade} = 1 - \frac{|X_k - M_k|}{X_k + M_k}$$

where: X_k = i's exports of industry k products to j
M_k = i's imports of industry k products from j

For the manufacturing sector as a whole, the index can be calculated as the weighted average of the degree of intra-industry trade for the industries that it comprises (Grubel and Lloyd, 1975).

Table 5.5 shows the indexes of Asian countries' intra-industry trade in the manufacturing sector for the years 1971 and 1986 (industries covered are SITC Sections 51 through 89 at the two-digit level). In most

Table 5.4 Estimation of specialization indexes

Dependent variables	Independent variables		
Specialization indexes	Per capita GNP	(Per capita GNP)²	$\bar{R}^2$
Primary commodities	−0.217 (−3.192)	–	0.326
Other manufactures	1.385 (2.014)	−0.08 (−1.803)	0.302
Machinery	0.318 (6.858)	–	0.708

Source: NRI.

93

Table 5.5 Indexes of intra-industry trade in manufacturing among Asian countries and USA

	Year	Japan	S. Korea	Taiwan	Hong Kong	Singapore	Thailand	Malaysia	Philippines	Indonesia
USA	71	0.373	0.191	0.247	0.225	0.356	0.130	0.019	0.103	0.019
	86	0.229	0.299	0.211	0.221	0.569	0.420	0.642	0.360	0.052
Japan	71		0.181	0.125	0.156	0.035	0.039	0.026	0.023	0.030
	86		0.365	0.261	0.232	0.226	0.173	0.336	0.210	0.071
S. Korea	71			0.154	0.309	0.189	0.109	0.016	0.027	0.052
	86			0.771	0.462	0.375	0.208	0.302	0.239	0.230
Taiwan	71				0.322	0.118	0.058	0.083	0.074	0.035
	86				0.163	0.348	0.202	0.336	0.181	0.080
Hong Kong	71					0.511	0.203	0.257	0.169	0.013
	86					0.702	0.501	0.432	0.368	0.276
Singapore	71						0.453	0.583	0.191	0.186
	86						0.436	0.769	0.507	0.200
Thailand	71							0.271	0.351	0.016
	86							0.583	0.311	0.198
Malaysia	71								0.131	0.346
	86								0.405	0.375
Philippines	71									0.031
	86									0.460

Source: NRI.

cases, the indexes rose sharply between 1971 and 1986, showing that intra-industry trade has grown rapidly in importance.

The index of intra-industry trade between two countries is expected to be positively related to their income levels and inversely related to their income gap: the higher their income levels, the higher will be manufactured goods' share of total exports; the smaller the income gap, the greater is the probability that they have similar trade structures (Linder, 1961). On the whole, the indexes of intra-industry trade are higher between Japan and the Asian NIEs than between Japan and the ASEAN countries. The indexes are also high among the Asian NIEs and among the ASEAN countries because the levels of development are similar within each group.

An exception to the above rule is that the index of intra-industry trade between Hong Kong and Taiwan was relatively low in 1986 and had actually declined since 1971. This exception is largely a reflection of the fact that trade between the two sides came to be dominated by re-exports to and from China. As the gap in the level of economic development suggests, trade between Taiwan and China consists mainly of the exchange of China's primary commodities with Taiwan's industrial products – a pattern typical between a developing country and an industrialized country. If re-export trade is excluded, the index of intra-industry trade between Hong Kong and Taiwan, which have similar income levels, should be much higher. This instance suggests that the intra-industry index may be biased when substantial re-export trade is involved.

Intra-industry trade between Japan and the Asian countries has grown in importance since the mid-1980s with rapid industrialization in the latter (Figure 5.6). The initial trend was the development of intra-industry trade between the Asian NIEs and Japan in metals (notably iron and steel), miscellaneous manufactured goods and textiles, followed more recently by that in machinery. Intra-industry trade between Japan and the ASEAN countries is in general less advanced but has been catching up at a very rapid pace. Indeed, the degree of intra-industry trade in electrical machinery and in precision instruments between Japan and the ASEAN countries has surpassed that between Japan and the Asian NIEs (See JETRO, 1992).

To confirm the relationship between intra-industry trade and income levels, the intra-industry trade index can be estimated as a function of the sum and the difference of two countries' per-capita incomes. Data for 1986 is used and the sample covers all combinations of countries in Table 5.5 except those involving Hong Kong and Singapore, whose

(1) Asian NIEs

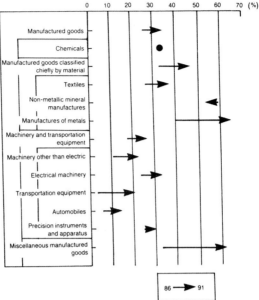

(2) ASEAN nations

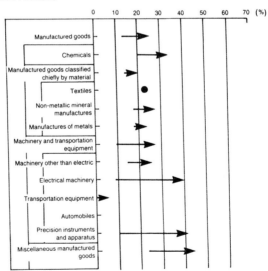

Figure 5.6 Japan-Asia intra-industry trade index by item
Note: Arrows indicate the change in the index of intra-industry trade as defined in the text from 1986 to 1991.
Source: JETRO (1992).

exports include substantial re-exports. The result can be summarized as follows

$$h = -0.65 + \underset{(3.97)}{0.58} \left(1 - \frac{|Y_i - Y_j|}{Y_i + Y_j}\right) + \underset{(2.01)}{0.08} \log(Y_i + Y_j)$$

$\bar{R}^2 = 0.423$ and figures in ( ) indicate t-values

where: h = index of intra-industry trade
Y_i = country i's per capita GNP
Y_j = country j's per capita GNP

The second and third terms on the right-hand side of the equation measure the degree of income equality (reciprocal of the income gap) and the sum of the income levels, respectively. Both coefficients are statistically significant at the 95 per cent confidence level, and as expected both carry the positive sign. In particular, the explanatory power of the degree of income equality is very high (Figure 5.7).

Intra-industry trade index

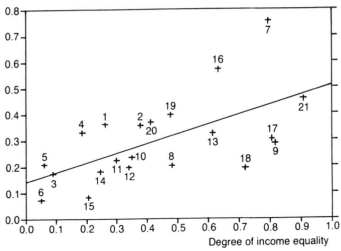

Figure 5.7 The degree of income equality and intra-industry trade
Note: The numbers denote the following combinations of countries: 1 Japan–Korea
2 Japan–Taiwan 3 Japan–Thailand 4 Japan–Malaysia 5 Japan–Philippines
6 Japan–Indonesia 7 Korea–Thailand 8 Korea–Thailand 9 Korea–Malaysia
10 Korea–Philippines 11 Korea–Indonesia 12 Taiwan–Thailand 13 Taiwan–Malaysia
14 Taiwan–Philippines 15 Taiwan–Indonesia 16 Thailand–Malaysia
17 Thailand–Philippines 18 Thailand–Indonesia 19 Malaysia–Philippines
20 Malaysia–Indonesia 21 Philippines–Indonesia.
Source: NRI.

Intra-industry trade among Asian countries is expected to continue to increase in the future as incomes rise and the income gap between the advanced countries and the developing countries shrinks. The result will be that a larger and larger share of intra-regional trade will be in manufactured goods instead of in primary commodities.

APPENDIX: TRADE STRUCTURE AND THE BALANCE-OF-PAYMENTS CYCLE

In the course of economic development, the trade balance usually deteriorates in the early phase, improves as income approaches the advanced country level, and deteriorates again at a later stage. This process forms the key relationship in the 'balance-of-payments cycle' described in Chapter 2. Our notion of the stages of trade structure in this chapter, coupled with the hypothesis that income elasticities depend on the commodity composition of trade, suggests a possible explanation for the evolution of the trade balance in the course of economic development.

Following Johnson (1958), the rate of change in the export/import ratio (an indicator of the trade balance) can be broken down into the income effect and the price effect. That is

$$r = \varepsilon_X Y^* - \varepsilon_M Y + (\eta_X + \eta_M - 1)(P_X - P_M)$$

where: r = rate of change in the export/import ratio

$\varepsilon_X(\varepsilon_M)$ = income elasticity of exports (imports)
$\eta_X(\eta_M)$ = price elasticity of exports (imports)
$Y^*(Y)$ = world (domestic) economic growth rate
$P_X(P_M)$ = rate of change in export (import) prices

Ignoring the price effect, and assuming that $Y^* = Y$, the equation simplifies to

$$r = (\varepsilon_X - \varepsilon_M)Y$$

Noting that the overall import (export) elasticity is equal to the weighted average of the import (export) elasticities of commodity components – primary commodities, other manufactures and machinery as defined above – and assuming that import and export elasticities are equal for the same category of goods, we have

$$\varepsilon_X = a_1\varepsilon_1 + a_2\varepsilon_2 + (1 - a_1 - a_2)\varepsilon_3$$
$$\text{and} \quad \varepsilon_M = b_1\varepsilon_1 + b_2\varepsilon_2 + (1 - b_1 - b_2)\varepsilon_3$$

where: $a_1(b_1)$ = primary commodities' share of exports (imports)

$a_2(b_2)$ = other manufactures' share of exports (imports)
ε_1 = income elasticity of primary commodities
ε_2 = income elasticity of other manufactures
ε_3 = income elasticity of machinery

and r can be written as:

$$r = [(a_1 - b_1)(\varepsilon_1 - \varepsilon_3) + (a_2 - b_2)(\varepsilon_2 - \varepsilon_3)]Y$$

Assuming that elasticity is highest for other manufactures and lowest for primary commodities, with machinery lying somewhere between, that is, $\varepsilon_2 > \varepsilon_3 > \varepsilon_1$, then

$$r > 0 \text{ if } (a_1 - b_1) < 0 \text{ and } (a_2 - b_2) > 0$$
$$\text{and } r < 0 \text{ if } (a_1 - b_1) > 0 \text{ and } (a_2 - b_2) < 0$$

At the early stage of economic development, comparative advantage lies in primary commodities, so that: $a_1 - b_1 > 0$ and $a_2 - b_2 < 0$. As a result, r is negative and the export/import ratio (balance of trade) declines (deteriorates). As industrialization reaches a higher level, $a_1 - b_1$ becomes negative, $a_2 - b_2$ becomes positive and the export/import ratio begins to rise. Finally, $a_2 - b_2$ begins to fall again as comparative advantage shifts from other manufactures to machinery and the export/import ratio may fall again when the deterioration in the trade balance of primary commodities and other manufactures outweighs the improvement in the trade balance of machinery.

This seems to correspond to the experience of the Asian NIEs that experienced substantial improvement in their trade balances when their trade structures were at the mature NIE stage (Korea, Taiwan and Hong Kong during the 1980s). Likewise, the recent deterioration in the trade balances of the ASEAN countries (which still have trade structures typical of developing countries) can also be explained by the disparity between import and export elasticities that results from the asymmetry in the commodity composition of exports and imports.

In the case of Japan, changing commodity composition of trade has led to a convergence of the income elasticities of exports and imports. The large gap between the two elasticities has been an important factor contributing to Japan's large trade imbalance, especially the trade surplus with the United States. Since 1986, though, the income elasticity of exports has declined, due to an increase in the share of capital goods in total exports, while the income elasticity of imports has risen, following an increase in the share of manufactured goods in total imports. As a result, the gap between the two elasticities has been diminishing (NRI, 1991).

6

DEEPENING
INTRA-REGIONAL
INTERDEPENDENCE

INTRODUCTION

Economic interdependence among the Asian countries has been deepening on the back of rising intra-regional trade and direct investment. The decline of US economic power and the ensuing intensification of trade friction have reduced the importance of the United States as the final destination for Asian exports. At the same time, the increase in foreign direct investment among the Asian countries has boosted intra-regional trade. The Asian countries are emerging as major trading partners for both Japan and the United States. This chapter first studies the changing regional composition of trade and the trade relations among the Asian NIEs, Japan and the United States in the context of the Pacific trade triangle. This is then followed by an analysis of the implications of these recent changes for the pattern of interdependence in the Pacific region.

THE CHANGING DIRECTION OF TRADE[1]

Rising intra-regional trade

Until the mid-1980s, trade in the Asia-Pacific region had been dominated by exports across the Pacific Ocean, but this pattern of trade flow has changed dramatically in the last few years. In line with the global trend toward regionalism, intra-regional trade among Asian-Pacific countries has increased sharply, while the relative importance of the United States as an export market for these countries has declined. In contrast, the share of US exports absorbed by the Asia-Pacific region – particularly the Asian NIEs – has started to grow.

A look at the degree of export dependence of the Asian countries (including Japan) broken down by region shows that the share of intra-regional trade rose from 30.9 per cent in 1986 to reach 43.1 per cent in 1992 (Table 6.1). In contrast, the share of the US market dropped from 34.1 per cent to 24.2 per cent over the same period. The shift of export destinations from the United States to the Asia-Pacific region is particularly marked for the Asian NIEs. Intra-regional trade's share of total NIEs export rose from 31.9 per cent to 43.5 per cent, while that of the United States slipped from 37.2 per cent to 24.2 per cent per cent between 1986 and 1992. For the ASEAN countries, the shift in the regional composition of trade has been less remarkable. Exports to Asia rose from 23.9 per cent in 1986 to 30.8 per cent in 1992, largely reflecting the rising share of the Asian NIEs, but the declining share of Japan kept the share of intra-regional trade broadly stable at around 52 per cent.

Asia has also emerged as Japan's largest export market (Figure 6.1). Japanese exports to Asia reached $112.2 billion in 1992, accounting for 33.0 per cent of total Japanese exports. Of this total, exports to the NIEs accounted for 21.4 per cent, exports to the ASEAN countries 8.1 per cent, and exports to China 3.5 per cent. For Japan, exports to Asia have now surpassed those to the United States, which amounted to $96.7 billion in 1992, accounting for 28.5 per cent of Japan's total exports.

For the United States, the Asia-Pacific region has become an important export market. The value of US exports to Japan, the Asian NIEs, ASEAN and China has surpassed that to the EC since 1986. The increase in NIEs-bound exports has been most impressive: by 1992, the value of US exports to the Asian NIEs surpassed that of US exports to Japan.

The determinants of the direction of exports

The major determinants of a country's export dependence on a partner country (defined as the partner country's share of total exports) are: (1) the partner country's share of world imports; (2) the complementarity between the country's export structure and the import structure of its trading partner and (3) bilateral trade barriers.

A country's import share in turn depends on: (1) its share of the world's real output (or GNP); (2) its real effective exchange rate; (3) its import prices relative to the world average and (4) trade barriers – both physical (such as absolute geographical distance from markets and the cost of the transportation necessary to overcome it) and artificial (such

101

Table 6.1 Asian countries' export dependence by region

Share of total exports, %

Exporter	Importer	1980	1985	1986	1987	1988	1989	1990	1991	1992
Asian NIEs	USA	24.8	34.8	37.2	35.1	31.3	29.7	27.0	24.5	24.2
	EC	16.4	10.3	12.3	13.9	14.3	13.8	15.4	15.6	13.6
	Japan	10.1	10.0	10.2	11.5	12.4	12.4	11.3	10.5	9.3
	Asian NIEs	9.7	8.9	9.0	9.6	10.8	11.4	12.5	13.6	14.3
	ASEAN	10.7	7.6	6.5	6.4	6.7	7.6	8.8	9.0	8.4
	China	2.0	7.2	6.1	6.8	8.1	8.1	7.9	9.4	11.5
	Asia	22.4	23.7	21.6	22.7	25.6	27.1	29.1	32.1	34.3
	Asia + Japan	32.5	33.7	31.9	34.2	38.1	39.5	40.5	42.5	43.5
ASEAN	USA	18.8	19.8	19.6	20.1	19.7	20.6	19.4	18.3	21.1
	EC	13.6	11.8	14.2	14.9	15.4	15.1	16.1	16.5	16.9
	Japan	34.5	31.0	27.6	26.0	24.6	24.3	24.4	22.9	22.0
	Asian NIEs	18.0	20.0	18.7	20.7	21.0	20.2	21.9	23.2	23.6
	ASEAN	3.2	4.5	3.7	3.9	3.6	4.1	4.2	4.0	4.5
	China	0.8	1.3	1.6	2.1	2.3	2.1	2.1	2.3	2.6
	Asia	22.1	25.7	23.9	26.7	27.0	26.5	28.2	29.5	30.8
	Asia + Japan	56.6	56.8	51.6	52.7	51.6	50.8	52.5	52.3	52.8
China	USA	5.4	8.5	8.5	7.7	7.1	8.5	8.7	8.8	10.7
	EC	13.1	8.4	12.9	9.9	10.0	9.4	9.7	9.7	10.3
	Japan	22.3	22.3	16.3	16.2	16.9	16.2	15.0	14.6	14.5
	Asian NIEs	26.4	33.7	35.3	38.2	41.5	45.5	48.3	51.9	53.0
	ASEAN	4.3	2.7	2.1	2.5	2.8	2.5	3.0	3.0	2.8
	Asia	30.7	36.4	37.4	40.7	44.3	48.1	51.3	54.9	55.8
	Asia + Japan	52.9	58.7	53.7	56.8	61.2	64.2	66.4	69.5	70.3

$$C_{ij} = \sum_k \left(\frac{X_{ik}}{X_i} \times \frac{M_{jk}}{M_j} \times \frac{M^*}{M_k^*} \right)$$

where: X_{ik} = i's exports of commodity k
X_i = i's total exports
M_{jk} = j's imports of commodity k
M_j = j's total imports
M_k^* = world imports of commodity k
M^* = world total imports

It should be noted that, measured as such, complementarity depends not only on the 'real' commodity composition of trade but also on the relative prices between different categories of imports or exports.[2] Thus, for example, a sharp increase in oil prices would raise ASEAN's export complementarity with Japan because it would raise primary commodities' share of ASEAN exports and Japanese imports at the same time.

Country bias favours the exports of one trading partner relative to another. Such bias may arise as a result of relative geographical proximity or import preference granted to specific countries. For example, the Asian NIEs – Hong Kong and Taiwan in particular – have benefited more than other countries from China's open-door policy. Similarly, recent market opening measures in Japan and the Asian NIEs (including action programmes to buy more from the United States) that aim to reduce bilateral trade imbalance (and trade friction) with the United States make these markets more easily accessible for US exports. On the other hand, the graduation of the Asian NIEs from the US GSP in 1989 should accelerate the downward trend of their dependence on the US market.

In order to verify the explanatory power of the above determinants of trade flow, the export dependence ratio (X_{ij}) of one country i on another country j can be estimated using time series data in the following form[3]

$$X_{ij} = a_0 + a_1 M_j + a_2 C_{ij} (+ a_3 B_{ij} + a_4 \text{ Dummy})$$

where: M_j = country j's share of world imports
C_{ij} = complementarity between country i's exports and country j's imports as defined above
B_{ij} = country i's imports from j / country i's exports to j

B indicates the size of the bilateral trade imbalance and is included as a proxy for country bias for equations involving the United States as an exporter. This factor takes into account the effect that Japan, for example, is likely to implement measures to promote imports from the

United States when the bilateral trade imbalance with the United States increases. In addition, for equations involving the Asian NIEs as exporters, a dummy has been included to take into account the effect of the open-door policy in China, which first emerged as a major export destination in the late 1970s.

The result, as summarized in Table 6.2, supports our explanation of the direction of exports. First, in all cases, the partner country's shares of world trade are statistically significant (at the 97.5 per cent confidence level) in explaining bilateral export dependence ratios. Second, except for US exports to the Asian NIEs, the complementarity index is also found to be a major determinant of the direction of trade. Third, the bilateral trade imbalance between the two sides of the Pacific, which has led to import liberalization measures in Japan and the Asian NIEs in favour of imports from the United States, is found to be important in explaining the rising share of US exports heading to Japan and the Asian NIEs. Finally, the 'China dummies' in the equations involving the Asian NIEs' export dependence on the United States and Japan are negative, suggesting that China's open-door policy has led to a diversion of the Asian NIEs' exports away from the United States and Japan.

THE PACIFIC TRADE TRIANGLE

In this section we take a closer look at the trade relations among the Asian NIEs, Japan and the United States in the context of the Pacific trade triangle. As there are already a number of studies on the direct trade link between Japan and the United States, we focus on the indirect link between Japan and the United States through the Asian NIEs.[4]

The growth in trade among these three regions has been spectacular (Figure 6.2). The value of trade in dollar terms multiplied 3.1 times since 1980 to reach $358 billion in 1992. Until 1987 trade expansion was led by the surge in Japanese and NIEs exports to the United States, which resulted in a large trade imbalance between the two sides of the Pacific. Subsequently, however, triangular trade has been led by rising US exports to the Asian NIEs and Japan on one hand, and Japanese exports to the Asian NIEs on the other. This has resulted in a reduction in the US trade deficit with the two regions, but a further widening of the trade imbalance between Japan and the Asian NIEs.

The traditional triangular trade relations among the Asian NIEs, Japan and the United States can be characterized by the Asian NIEs' heavy dependence on Japan for capital and intermediate goods on the input side, and on the United States as a market on the output side.

Table 6.2 Estimation of export dependence ratios

Exporter	Importer	Constant	Importer's share of world imports	Complementarity index	Trade imbalance	China dummy	$\bar{R}^2$	D.W.
Japan	US	−0.22	1.75 (5.78)	0.23 (4.00)	–	–	0.956	1.31
	NIEs	−0.21	0.71 (2.76)	0.32 (2.41)	–	–	0.568	0.85
US	Japan	−0.24	1.55 (4.73)	0.24 (6.99)	0.015 (6.67)	–	0.811	2.27
	NIEs	−0.04	1.32 (10.79)	0.04 (0.63)	0.004 (1.82)	–	0.976	2.45
NIEs	Japan	−0.32	1.78 (2.34)	0.44 (4.47)	–	−0.0027 (−2.62)	0.628	2.29
	US	−0.37	1.64 (4.58)	0.43 (2.19)	–	−0.0047 (−2.05)	0.843	2.07

Notes: 1 Sample period: 1972–88. 2 Figures in ( ) denote t-values. 3 Trade imbalance between USA and the Asian NIEs lagged by 1 period. 4 China dummy takes the value 0 for the years 1972 to 1979 and 1,2,3 ......9 for 1980 to 1988.
Source: NRI.

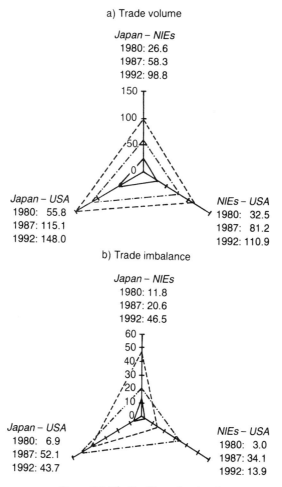

Figure 6.2 The Pacific trade triangle
Note: Figures denote respective totals of bilateral trade in Part a) and bilateral trade
imbalances in Part b) for 1980, 1987 and 1992 ($ bil).
Source: US Department of Commerce and Japanese Ministry of Finance.

Japan's share of Asian NIEs imports reached 26.7 per cent at its peak in
1986 while the US share of NIEs' exports was as high as 37.2 per cent.
Indeed, until 1988, imports of the Asian NIEs from Japan had followed
closely trends in their exports to the United States (Figure 6.3). The
sharp rise in Asian NIEs exports accompanying the yen's sharp
appreciation between 1986 and 1987, for example, was accompanied

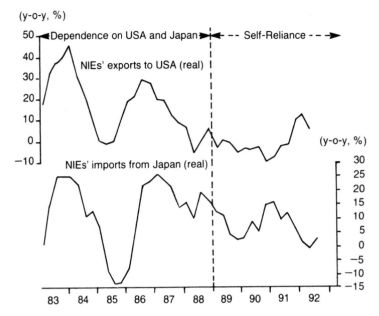

Figure 6.3 The weakening Japan-NIEs-USA link

Notes: 1 Hong Kong exports exclude re-exports. 2 NIEs' imports from Japan based on Japanese trade statistics. 3 NIEs' exports to USA deflated by unit value of overall NIEs' exports and NIEs' imports from Japan deflated by unit value of overall Japanese exports.

Source: Compiled by NRI based on NIEs' and Japanese trade statistics.

by a surge in Asian NIEs imports from Japan. The increase in the Asian NIEs' trade surplus with the United States also synchronized with an increase in its trade deficit with Japan. This relation was so close that Japan was criticized for exporting to the United States indirectly through their subsidiaries in the Asian NIEs.

The linkage between Japan and the United States through the Asian NIEs, however, has weakened in the last few years. The recovery in NIEs' imports from Japan in 1990 was not accompanied by a strengthening of NIEs' exports to the United States, and the slowdown in NIEs' imports from Japan since early 1991 has actually been accompanied by a rebound in NIEs' exports to the United States.

The fading of the traditional pattern reflects declines in the Asian NIEs' dependence on Japan as a supplier of capital goods and on the United States as a market for their products. NIEs' imports from Japan as a percentage of their GNP dropped from 13.2 per cent in 1988 to 11.4 per cent in 1991, as a larger proportion of capital goods and

109

intermediate goods can now be procured from alternative sources in both the domestic market and other Asian countries. Total exports as a per centage of GNP dropped from 51.6 per cent in 1987 to 40.5 per cent in 1991, reflecting the growing size of the domestic market, and the US share of NIEs' total exports dropped from 37.2 per cent in 1986 to 24.2 per cent in 1992.

While Japan's indirect link with the United States through the Asian NIEs has been weakening, a new trade triangle linking the Asian NIEs to the United States through China has emerged (Figure 6.4). This largely reflects the large-scale relocation of production facilities from Hong Kong and Taiwan to southern China, as we have seen in Chapter 2. While exports of Hong Kong and Taiwan to the United States have stagnated since 1987, China expanded its exports to United States by four times between 1987 and 1992 (according to US statistics). The combined share of the three countries, or Greater China, of US imports edged up from 10.0 per cent to 11.3 per cent in 1992.

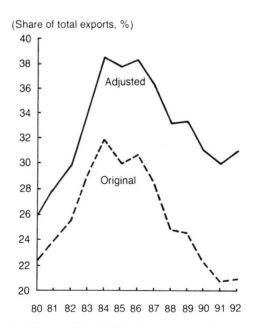

(Share of total exports, %)

Figure 6.4 Greater China's falling dependence on the US market
Note: Adjusted series shows US share of Greater China's total exports when trade among China, Hong Kong and Taiwan is excluded from total exports.
Source: Customs statistics of China, Hong Kong and Taiwan.

This, however, does not imply that Greater China's dependence on the US market has increased, as their exports to other markets have expanded at a even faster pace. The US share of the three countries' total exports dropped from a peak level of 31.8 per cent in 1984 to 20.9 per cent in 1992, according to customs statistics of the export side. This way of calculation may under-estimate the share of the United States on the ground that figures for total exports include substantial trade in intermediate goods among the three regions themselves (notably through Hong Kong). A clearer picture emerges if we consider China, Taiwan and Hong Kong as a single country and exclude trade among themselves in total exports. The US share of their exports so calculated also dropped from 38.5 per cent in 1984 to 30.9 per cent in 1992. Although the divergence between the two sets of figures has increased in recent years reflecting growing trade among the three countries, the conclusion that the dependence of Greater China on the US market has fallen sharply remains robust.

IMPLICATIONS FOR THE PATTERN OF MACROECONOMIC INTERDEPENDENCE

The drastic changes in the direction of trade and investment have dominant effects on the pattern of macroeconomic interdependence in the Asia-Pacific region. In what follows we illustrate this point with two examples: (1) the desynchronization between Asian and US economic growth rates and (2) the interdependence between Japan and the Asian NIEs through the yen–dollar rate. While the former focuses on the income effect of transmission of economic fluctuations, the latter places more emphasis on the price effect.

Desynchronization between Asian and US economic growth rates

The diminishing influence of the United States on the Asian economies can be confirmed by noting that economic growth rates on the two sides of the Pacific no longer synchronize with each other – a trend which has become more and more apparent in the last few years (Figure 6.5).

The impact of US economic growth rate on the Asian countries can be analysed by calculating the elasticity of Asian economic growth with respect to US economic growth. Let Y denote the Asian economic growth rate and U denote the US growth rate. The elasticity ε is defined as

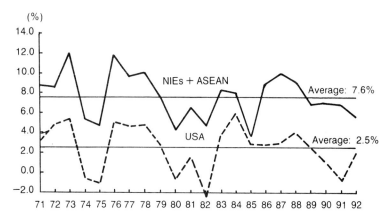

Figure 6.5 Desynchronization of Asian and US growth rates
Source: IMF, *International Financial Statistics.*

$$\varepsilon = \frac{dY/Y}{dU/U}$$

Conceptually, ε can be decomposed into three components. That is

$$\varepsilon = \frac{dY/Y}{dU/U} = \frac{dY/Y}{dX/X} \times \frac{dX/X}{\cdot dV/V} \times \frac{dV/V}{dU/U}$$

where X denotes total Asian exports and V denotes Asian exports to the United States. The three terms on the right correspond, respectively, to (1) Asia's export multiplier in elasticity form, (2) US share of Asian exports, and (3) the income elasticity of US demand for Asian exports. The magnitude of the elasticity therefore depends on the size of these three components. All three factors seem to suggest a falling elasticity of Asian economic growth with respect to US economic growth over time.

The first term can be broken down further to the export multiplier and exports' share of national income. The export multiplier depends on the Asian countries' marginal propensity to import and marginal propensity to save, according to the standard textbook version of the Keynesian model. A larger marginal propensity to save or marginal propensity to import implies larger leakage of demand on domestic goods and thus a lower exports multiplier. Both propensities seem to be rising in recent years in the Asian countries, suggesting that the exports multiplier is declining. Meanwhile, exports' share of national income in the Asian countries has also been falling, reflecting the growing importance of domestic markets.

The second term is equivalent to the US share of Asia's total exports (given $dX/dV=1$), which as we have seen before, has been falling sharply in recent years.

The third term shows the income elasticity of US demand for Asian exports (or income elasticity of US imports from Asia). Its magnitude depends, among other things on the domestic production capacity relative to demand. The US income elasticity of imports seems to have been falling recently alongside progress in industrial restructuring.

The elasticity ε can be estimated directly by regressing the Asian economic growth rate on the US economic growth rate, or by first estimating its three components separately and then deriving the elasticity from its components. While the former is easy to estimate, the latter requires an explicit model which includes a bilateral import-export function. Both methods can be criticized as partial analysis which neglects all other variables. The direct method may overestimate the elasticity as it may include the effect of economic growth in third countries that correlates with the US rate. The indirect method, on the other hand, may underestimate the elasticity as the indirect effects through third countries are totally ignored.

With these limitations in mind, and for the sake of simplicity, we use the direct method and estimate the elasticity in the following form

$$Y = a + bU,$$

The parameter b measures the elasticity of Asian economic growth with respect to world economic growth, while the constant term a shows the level of Asian economic growth determined independently of the world economic growth rate. To trace the shift in the elasticity over time, we repeat our estimation for the periods 1971–80, 1972–81, ..., 1983–92. The values of a and b corresponding to different estimation periods are shown in Figure 6.6.

The results of estimation confirm our contention that the link between US and Asian growth rates has been weakening. In the 1970s, a 1.0 per cent increase in the US economic rate tended to raise that of Asia (NIEs + ASEAN) by 1.0 per cent. Subsequently, it has followed a downward trend, falling to around 0.3 per cent recently.

In contrast to the Asian NIEs and the ASEAN countries, China's economic growth rate has come to be more dependent on the US economic growth rate. Repeating the above exercise using China instead of NIEs plus ASEAN as the dependent variable shows that the elasticity of Chinese growth with respect to US growth has risen from around zero to nearly 1.3 recently (Figure 6.7). This to a large extent

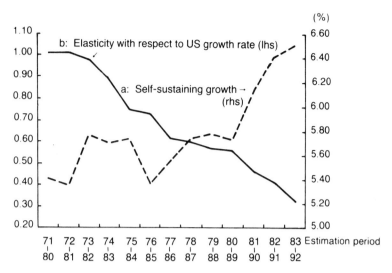

Figure 6.6 Weakening link between Asian and US growth rates
Note: Asia excludes China.
Source: NRI.

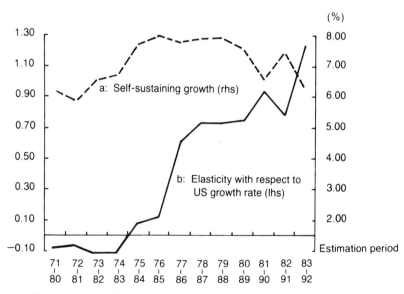

Figure 6.7 Strengthening link between Chinese and US growth rates
Source: NRI.

reflects the rising dependence of China on the United States as an export market.

The Asian NIEs as a built-in stabilizer of Japanese exports[5]

As Japan's dependence on the Asian market keeps rising, traditional economic relations characterized by the unilateral dependence of the Asian countries on Japan are giving way to interdependence between both sides. Economic growth in the neighbouring countries, the NIEs in particular, can no longer be neglected when discussing Japan's macroeconomic performance.

Japanese exports to the Asian NIEs have followed closely movements

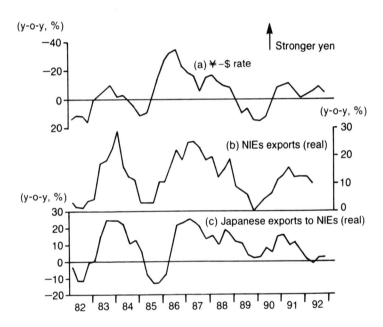

Figure 6.8 Yen–dollar rate and NIEs-Japan interdependence

Notes: 1 Japanese exports to NIEs deflated by unit value of overall Japanese exports
2 Estimation of Japanese exports to NIEs

$$\log (J) = 11.02 + 0.015(\text{time trend}) - 0.393 \log (\yen)$$
$$(14.59) \qquad\qquad (-6.07)$$

Sample period 1979Q3–1992Q4. Figures in brackets denote t-values. Shiller logs used in estimation.
$\bar{R}^2 = 0.965$ D.W. $= 0.387$

Source: Compiled by NRI based on customs-cleared statistics of Japan and the Asian NIEs.

115

in the yen–dollar rate and the Asian NIEs' export growth (Figure 6.8). Japanese exports to the NIEs surged between 1986–8 against a background of an export boom in the Asian NIEs themselves, which resulted from the yen's sharp appreciation against the dollar. The situation was reversed between 1989 and mid-1990 when the yen depreciated against the dollar. The rebound of the yen since mid-1990 has again been accompanied by a recovery in the NIEs' exports and Japanese exports to the Asian NIEs.

The relations between the yen–dollar rate and Japanese exports to the Asian NIEs can be explained by examining the link between the yen–dollar rate and the Asian NIEs' export growth rate (Figure 6.8a and b), and then that between the NIEs' export growth rate and Japanese exports to the Asian NIEs (Figure 6.8b and c). As explained in Chapter 3, the Asian NIEs are competitors of Japan in international markets, and their currencies are loosely pegged to the dollar. An appreciation of the yen, for example, by driving up Japanese export prices in dollar terms, boosts the Asian NIEs' exports, not only in Japan, but also in other countries. This occurs either through an improvement in price competitiveness if the Asian NIEs maintain their export prices or through an improvement in export profits if they follow Japan in raising their export prices. On the other hand, in order to expand exports, the Asian NIEs have to import capital and intermediate goods (including parts and components) from Japan. This reflects the high complementarity between Japanese exports and the NIEs' imports (or the dependence of the Asian NIEs on Japan). An appreciation of the yen therefore boosts Japanese exports to the Asian NIEs indirectly through this income effect. Theoretically, an appreciation of the yen should curb exports to the Asian NIEs through the negative price effect, but the effect here is very small because Japanese exports are composed mainly of goods that cannot be produced domestically in the Asian NIEs.

In contrast to exports to the Asian NIEs, Japanese exports to other major markets (the United States and the EC, for example) are more responsive to changes in prices. When the yen appreciates, exports to these markets tend to slow down. Exports to the Asian NIEs thus act as a built-in stabilizer for total Japanese exports, partly offsetting the declines in overall exports as the yen appreciates and the increases as the yen depreciates.

Reflecting the asymmetric impact of the yen's fluctuation on Japanese exports to the Asian NIEs and to other markets, the Asian NIEs' share of Japanese exports tends to rise when the yen appreciates and decline when the yen depreciates (Figure 6.9). In addition to the

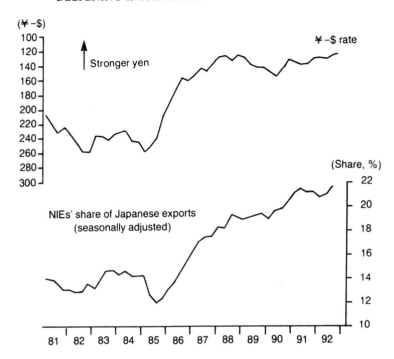

Figure 6.9 Yen–dollar rate and NIEs' share of Japanese exports
Note: Estimation of NIEs' share of Japanese exports:

log (Share) = 3.9435 + 0.0016(time trend) − 0.2923 log(yen–dollar rate)
(4.77)   −(3.75)

Sample period 1981Q1 to 1992Q3. Figures in parentheses denote t-values.
$\bar{R}^2 = 0.864$ D.W. = 0.293

Source: Compiled by NRI based on IMF, *International Financial Statistics* and Japanese customs-cleared statistics.

cyclical fluctuation caused by the exchange-rate factor, the Asian NIEs' share of Japanese exports has followed an upward trend, reflecting the growing share of the Asian NIEs in total world imports. Simple regression shows that a 1.0 per cent depreciation (appreciation) of the yen–dollar rate tends to reduce (raise) the Asian NIEs' share of Japanese exports by 0.29 per cent.[6] The reverse side of the coin is that a 1.0 per cent depreciation (appreciation) of the yen tends to increase (reduce) the share of the rest of the world by the same amount.

The trade relations between Japan and the Asian NIEs can be formalized as follows. (The rest of this section is a bit technical and can be skipped without affecting the flow of our arguments.)

Real exports of the Asian NIEs, N, can be formulated as a function of the yen–dollar rate ¥. That is

$$N = N(¥) \tag{1}$$

with $dN/d¥ < 0$. That is, a depreciation of the yen leads to lower exports in the Asian NIEs.

Likewise, Japanese exports to the Asian NIEs (in real terms), J, can be formulated as a function of the yen–dollar rate, and total NIEs exports

$$J = J(N, ¥) \tag{2}$$

with $\partial J/\partial N > 0$ and $\partial J/\partial ¥ > 0$. That is, Japanese exports to the Asian NIEs rise with an increase in NIEs' exports (positive income effect) and with a depreciation of the yen against the dollar (negative price effect).

Substituting (1) into (2) gives

$$J = J(N(¥), ¥) \tag{3}$$

so that

$$dJ/d¥ = \partial J/\partial N \times dN/d¥ + \partial J/\partial ¥.$$

The hypothesis we want to test is that a depreciation of the yen (a larger value for ¥) leads to lower Japanese exports to the Asian NIEs, or $dJ/d¥ < 0$. This requires that the indirect effect through the income effect ($\partial J/\partial N \times dN/d¥$) be larger than the direct effect ($\partial J/\partial ¥$) through the price effect (both measured in absolute terms).

Our model can now be tested by estimating equation (3). The results, as summarized in Figure 6.8, show that a 1.0 per cent depreciation (appreciation) of the yen tends to reduce (raise) Japanese exports to the Asian NIEs by 0.39 per cent. With the Asian NIEs now absorbing about 20 per cent of total Japanese exports, a 1.0 per cent appreciation in the yen rate against the dollar tends to raise total Japanese exports by 0.078 per cent ($0.39 \times 20\%$) through this built-in stabilizing effect. This supports our hypothesis that the Asian NIEs act as a built-in stabilizer for Japanese exports.

The growing importance of the Asian NIEs for Japan as an export market suggests that this built-in stabilizing effect may become even more significant in the future. This, however, has to be qualified by the fact that complementarity between Japanese exports and NIEs' imports may decline as industrialization in the Asian NIEs reaches a higher stage so that Japanese exports to the Asian NIEs may become more and more price elastic.

7

EXPANSION OF NEW FRONTIERS

INTRODUCTION[1]

So far we have focused on the interdependence of the traditional high-growth economies. In this chapter, we examine the expansion of their new frontiers, which is helping to integrate the socialist countries into the regional economy. This trend has been promoted by the end of the Cold War and economic reform and open-door policy of the socialist countries in the region (notably China) on one hand, and growing complementarity in the economic structures of countries on both sides of the new frontiers on the other. In this chapter we start by summarizing the economic reform and open-door policy in Asia's socialist countries. This is followed by an analysis of how economic cooperation through the exploitation of complementarity in economic structures can benefit the countries involved. Finally, we conclude this chapter by studying the emergence of regional economic zones and recent developments in multilateral cooperation among Asian countries.

ECONOMIC REFORM AND OPEN-DOOR POLICY IN THE SOCIALIST COUNTRIES

The reverse domino phenomenon

The global trend towards detente, by removing the political barriers separating socialist countries and market economies, has helped make cooperation across national borders possible in Asia. Recent events in Eastern Europe and the former Soviet Union, in particular, will have long-term effects on the socialist countries in the region. The failure of Soviet-type socialism as a model of economic development contrasts sharply with the success of the Asian NIEs and ASEAN which have relied mainly on the market in organizing economic activities. With the age of ideology closing and aid from the former East Bloc countries drying up, the time is ripe for the socialist countries in Asia to reconsider their development strategy. An obvious alternative is to open their doors further to take advantage of the dynamism in the Asia-Pacific region.

During the 1960s, at the height of the Cold War, the famous domino theory predicted that if Vietnam fell to communism, the rest of Southeast Asia would follow. Ironically, the reverse is now taking place, with the expansion of new frontiers of the Asian economies into the socialist countries gathering momentum (Figure 7.1).

China: the dragon in metamorphosis

China's economic growth since it adopted the reform and open-door policy in the late 1970s has been impressive. The average annual economic growth reached 8.5 per cent between 1979 and 1992, one of

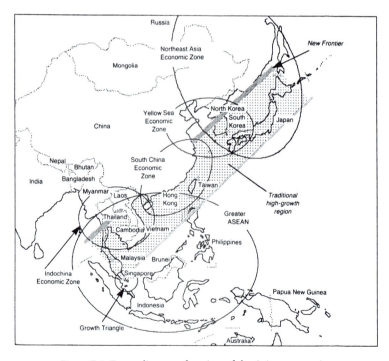

Figure 7.1 Expanding new frontiers of the Asian economics
Source: NRI.

120

the highest among the Asian countries during the same period. Exports multiplied over six times between 1979 and 1992 to reach $85 billion (Figure 7.2).

The following factors seem to have contributed to the success of economic reform in China. First, reform has followed a gradual and step-by-step approach, as in the case of liberalization of price controls. This contrasts with the shock therapy pursued in Russia and in some other former East Bloc countries. Second, reforms in the agricultural sector preceded those in the industrial sector. Improved productivity in the agricultural sector with the dissolution of the communes freed China's 1.1 billion people from the threat of hunger, and this in turn helped promote political stability. Third, reform of the domestic

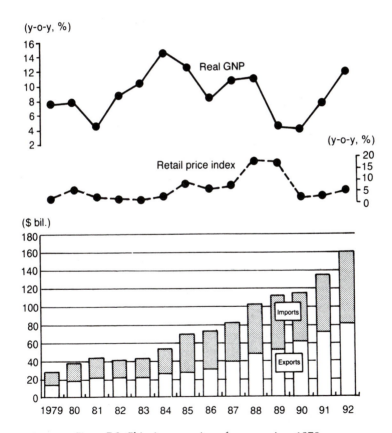

Figure 7.2 China's economic performance since 1979
Source: Compiled by NRI based on official statistics.

economy has been supplemented by an open-door policy that emphasizes export promotion and the inflow of foreign direct investment.

Since the beginning of 1992, China has stepped up its economic reform and open-door policy.[2] At the fourteenth National Congress of the Chinese Communist Party held in October 1992, the idea of 'a socialist market economy' was authorized and a leadership reshuffle was made for the smooth execution of new plans and policies. The socialist market economy envisioned by China is essentially the same as the market economies of the developed countries. Administrative intervention in China will henceforth be aimed mostly at preventing market failures.

At the same time, China has been extending its open-door policy from the coastal areas to other regions. Major cities along national borders and the Yangtze River were granted the right to extend preferential treatment to foreign capital in 1992. The government intends to turn these cities into economic hubs and step up the economic development in peripheral areas.

The accelerating liberalization of the Chinese economy has been followed by a rapid increase in foreign direct investment. In 1992 the inflow of foreign direct investment reached $58.5 billion (on a commitment basis), surpassing the cumulative value between 1979–91. Recent foreign direct investment in China has been characterized by an increase in large-scale investment projects and expansion to new business areas, such as banking, insurance, commerce, real estate and big resort development projects. At the same time wholly-owned foreign investment has risen, and investment to inland regions has expanded.

The introduction of foreign capital not only enhances China's export capacity but also helps improve corporate management efficiency. By opening up its domestic market to foreign companies, China aims to promote productivity through competition not only among Chinese enterprises but also with foreign companies.

China's economic reform and open-door policy have passed the point of 'no return'. Whether China will be able to continue its robust economic growth, however, will depend on how it can cope with structural problems such as poor performance of state-run enterprises and huge government fiscal deficits. China intends to solve these problems by shifting to the market economy. This process will prompt the reform of state-owned enterprises and thus reduce need for the government to cover its deficits. It will also help slash price subsidies through decontrol of prices.

China's transformation to a market economy and opening to the world will have a major effect on neighbouring countries. First, China is now a a model to follow for socialist countries in the region, helping to accelerate the reverse domino phenomenon. Second, the Asian NIEs, which are more developed than China, should benefit from expanding investment and trade with China. Third, risks from the return of Hong Kong to China in 1997 should be greatly reduced due to the virtual economic integration of China and Hong Kong. Fourth, the ASEAN countries may find China emerging as a tough competitor not only for export markets but also for direct foreign investment.

Vietnam: from war zone to trade zone

In Vietnam, the transition to a market economy started in late 1986 with the introduction of the Doi Moi policy. Much has been achieved in reducing inflation, in cutting fiscal deficits and in boosting agricultural production. Indeed, Vietnam has become the world's third largest exporter of rice. The country has also strengthened links with its neighbours through trade and investment. Constrained by the US trade embargo and the drying up of foreign aid from the former East Bloc countries, however, economic growth still lags far behind its neighbours.

Vietnam's relations with the United States are improving following the end of the civil war in Cambodia. The partial lifting of the US trade embargo on Vietnam in late 1992 is expected to be followed by more fully-fledged measures. The resumption of official development aid and direct investment from the industrial countries, the United States and Japan in particular, will help to speed up Vietnam's transition from a war zone to a trade zone. At the same time, private capital from overseas Vietnamese who fled the country after the Vietnam War and overseas Chinese will play an important role in the reconstruction of the Vietnamese economy.

North Korea: the last domino

North Korea has so far maintained an orthodox Soviet-type planned economy, which has resulted in stagnation and a widening income gap with South Korea. The recent sharp fall in official aid from the former Communist Bloc has brought the North Korean economy to the verge of collapse. Before the Korean War, the North had a higher level of economic development than the South, but today, South Korea's per capita GNP is about five times that of North Korea. With a population twice that of the North, South Korea's GNP is estimated at about ten times that of the North. This gap in economic power is comparable to the gap between the two Germanies before unification in 1990.

North Korea now faces the need to revitalize its economy by the introduction of foreign capital, as China did in the second half of the 1970s. Conditions for a more open economy are already falling into place as both North and South Korea take up UN membership and North Korea's previously icy relations with Japan and the United States have begun to thaw (Figure 7.3). At the same time, the relations between North and South Korea are changing, from confrontation to constructive dialogue, with less emphasis on political rhetoric and more on the 'nitty-gritty' of economic cooperation.

North Korea has already started opening its economy to the West. The government has announced plans to establish two free trade zones at the ports of Songbong and Rajin at the mouth of the Tumen River bordering China and Russia. North Korea hopes to attract foreign capital into these two free trade zones by combining them with the Tumen River Development Project to be discussed below.

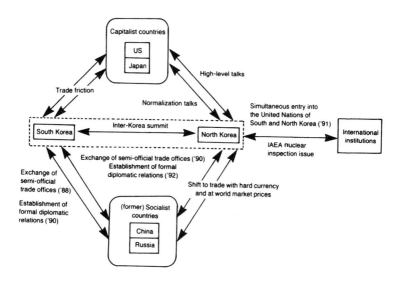

Figure 7.3 International relations of South and North Korea
Source: NRI.

124

GROWING ECONOMIC COMPLEMENTARITY ACROSS NEW FRONTIERS

The gains from economic cooperation for countries on both sides of the new frontiers – a form of peace dividend in Asia – can be immense.[3] Complementarity between the two sides of the new frontiers has increased in recent years, raising the potential gain from regional cooperation. Ironically, growing complementarity has resulted from the widening income gap between countries on the two sides of the new frontiers. Countries on the more advanced side of the frontiers have found that rapid economic growth pushes up wages and land prices. As a result, relocating their industries in neighbouring countries helps reduce production costs and enhance export competitiveness. For countries on the other side of the frontiers, the inflow of foreign direct investment provides them with employment opportunities, and the funds, technology and infrastructure needed for economic development. (The rest of this section is a bit technical and can be skipped without affecting the flow of our arguments.)

The effect of frontier expansion on the economic welfare of the countries involved can be illustrated by the textbook version of the theory of foreign direct investment (MacDougall, 1958). As a first approximation, the expansion of new frontiers can be treated conceptually as the relocation of capital stock from a capital-abundant country where the rate of return (which reflects the marginal productivity of capital) is low to one where the marginal productivity of capital is high. The investing country usually has a higher level of economic development than that of the receiving country.

Consider Country A (for example, Hong Kong) and Country B (for example, China) producing an identical output, using labour and capital. The labour force is assumed to be fixed in each country and fully employed. Assuming that perfect competition prevails in both countries, the returns on capital and labour are equal to their marginal products, both measured in terms of the output. In Figure 7.4, the vertical axis measures the marginal product of capital. The horizontal axis measures the capital stock in each country, measured from O for Country A and from O' for Country B, so that OO' measures the total capital stock of the two countries. AB and A'B' show the marginal product of capital for Country A and country B, respectively. Both schedules decline as the capital stock increases, reflecting diminishing marginal productivity, given fixed labour input.

In the absence of international factor mobility, Country A holds OC

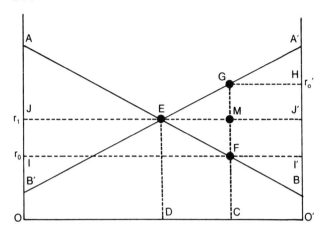

Figure 7.4 Output and welfare effect of frontier expansion
Source: NRI.

of capital and Country B holds O'C. The marginal products of capital (which equals to the return of capital) for Countries A and B are given by r_0 and r_0', respectively, with capital earning higher return in country B than country A. The income or output for Country A (Country B) is given by OAFC (O'CGA'), with OIFC (O'CGH) accruing to capital owners and IAF (HA'G) accruing to labour. In the absence of factor mobility across national borders, the concept of output (or GDP) coincides with income (or GNP).

Now let us assume that restrictions on capital flows between the two countries are removed (but labour mobility remains restricted). Investors in Country A will move capital to B where the return is higher until the returns in both countries become equal. This would require moving DC of capital from Country A to Country B. At equilibrium, Country A holds OD of capital while Country B holds O'D, both earning a return equal to r_1.[4] Output declines in Country A but rises in Country B, but income rises in both countries. Country A's GDP falls by DEFC, reflecting the decline in capital stock. However, this does not mean a decline in Country A's GNP as returns to investment in Country B as measured by DEMC more than offset the decline in domestic output. The net gain to Country A is given by EMF. On the other hand, Country B's GDP rises by DEGC, reflecting the rise in capital stock, but GNP increases only by EGM, as DEMC accrues to investors in Country A. GNP exceeds GDP by DEMC in Country A and the reverse is true for Country B. The increase in combined GDP (or GNP) of Country A and

Country B, which results from the improvement in the allocative efficiency of the capital stock, equals EGF.

The relocation of capital stock across national borders also alters the distribution of income between labour and capital in both countries. Although the income to be shared by labour and capital increases in both investing and receiving countries, labour-income falls in absolute terms in the former and capital-income drops in the latter. In Country A, where the capital/labour ratio declines, labour income falls by IJEF; capital-income rises by IJMF, IJEF at the expense of labour-income, and EMF gain from improved efficiency. In Country B, where the capital/labour ratio rises, labour-income rises by EGHJ', MGHJ' at the expense of capital income and EGM gain from improved efficiency.

EMERGING ECONOMIC ZONES AND REGIONAL INTEGRATION

The expansion of Asia's new frontiers is creating economic zones encompassing countries with different economic and political systems and at various stages of economic development. In addition to the 'South China Economic Zone' centring around Hong Kong, concepts of regional cooperation at more embryonic stages have emerged. They include the 'Northeast Asia Economic Zone' (comprising Japan, the Korean Peninsula, northern China and Far East Russia), 'Greater ASEAN' (comprising the six current members of ASEAN and the socialist countries in Indochina), and the 'Growth Triangle' encompassing Singapore and neighbouring provinces in Indonesia and Malaysia. These interlocking economic zones form a corridor linking fast-growing economies from the north to the south along the Western Pacific Rim.

'The South China Economic Zone'

The expansion of Asia's new frontiers is most apparent in southern China, which is emerging as a major production base for labour-intensive manufactured goods thanks to large-scale inflows of direct investment from Hong Kong. At first these investments were concentrated in the four Special Economic Zones (Shenzhen, Zhuhai, Shantou and Xiamen) set up in 1980, but gradually they spread inland to take advantage of even lower labour costs and looser regulations. Labour costs in southern China inside the special economic zones are one-fifth those in Hong Kong while those outside the zones are a mere one-tenth.

In most cases, cooperation between the two sides takes the form of outward processing. Hong Kong firms supply all necessary machinery, parts and raw materials to manufacturers in China and take care of the marketing of finished products. Partners in China provide land and labour and receive payment in the form of processing fees. The number of employees working for Hong Kong subcontractors, joint ventures or subsidiaries in Guangdong Province is estimated at more than 3 million. Hong Kong capital is also helping to build infrastructure in southern China, including a highway network linking Hong Kong, Guangzhou and Macao.

Reflecting these developments, the share of re-exports in Hong Kong's total exports rose from around 20 per cent in the mid-1970s to 75 per cent in 1992 (Figure 7.5). About 90 per cent of Hong Kong's re-exports involve China either as a source or a destination. Indeed, China has replaced the United States as Hong Kong's largest export market, and as a result, Hong Kong's economic growth now follows Chinese economic trends more closely than those of the United States (Figure 7.6). Economic integration between Hong Kong and southern China is also apparent in the monetary sphere: the Hong Kong dollar is now

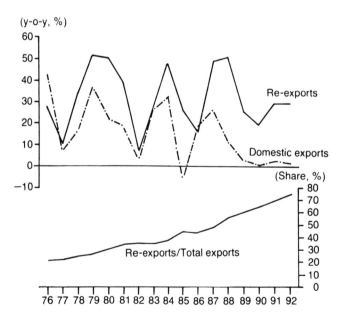

Figure 7.5 Growing importance of Hong Kong's re-exports
Source: Compiled by NRI based on Hong Kong trade statistics.

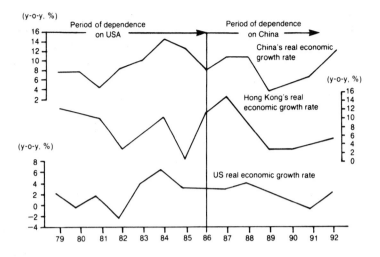

Figure 7.6 China replacing USA as Hong Kong's engine of economic growth
Source: Compiled by NRI based on official statistics.

widely circulated in Guangdong Province. The political border between Hong Kong and China will not disappear until 1997 but the economic border has already disappeared with the expansion of Hong Kong's economic frontier into China.[5]

Massive investment by Hong Kong companies in southern China has led to a large gap between Hong Kong's GDP and GNP. For Hong Kong companies, southern China can be likened to a newly discovered gold mine. Profits earned there are estimated at $10 billion, more than 10 per cent of Hong Kong's Gross Domestic Product (GDP). When this factor is taken into consideration, Hong Kong's economic growth rate in 1992 in terms of Gross National Product (GNP) is estimated to be about 2.0 percentage points higher than that measured in terms of GDP.[6]

Hong Kong's new relations with China, however, have also brought undesirable side effects to the domestic economy, such as de-industrialization and a sharp appreciation of the real exchange rate – symptoms similar to the Dutch disease. (See Appendix at the end of this chapter.) The number of workers in Hong Kong's manufacturing sector contracted by more than 30 per cent from a peak level of 870,000 in 1987 to 587,000 in the second quarter of 1992. The share of manufacturing in GNP dropped from 24.1 per cent in 1984 to 15.5 per cent in 1991. Inflation, as measured by the year-on-year increase in the CPI has stayed at around 10 per cent since 1989. Because the exchange rate of the Hong Kong dollar is pegged to the US dollar, the competitiveness of Hong Kong's domestic exports has declined, helping accelerate the process of de-industrialization.

In the last few years, Taiwanese manufacturers have also been expanding their investment in southern China, notably Fujian Province. Reflecting rising indirect exports to China, Taiwan's trade surplus with Hong Kong exceeded its trade surplus with the United States in 1992, reaching $13.6 billion. Taiwan's move in 1992 to allow its companies to invest directly in the mainland without setting up subsidiaries in third countries is paving the way for direct trade across the Taiwan Straits. Like Hong Kong companies before them, more and more Taiwanese companies will use China as an offshore production base for the manufacture of labour-intensive products.

Through investment and trade, the economic integration of Hong Kong, Taiwan and southern China is accelerating. Hong Kong, Taiwan, Guangdong and Fujian Provinces have a combined population of 115 million and a total GNP of $300 billion which is comparable to the size of ASEAN. Hong Kong is taking advantage of its free-port position and is emerging as the region's trading and financial centre. Indeed, it has become the world's second largest container port after Singapore and the tenth leading exporter. With southern China as its hinterland, Hong Kong is fast transforming itself from a city-state to the capital city of a national economy. Boosted by Hong Kong and Taiwanese capital, southern China has entered a stage of economic takeoff, and Guangdong Province now boasts the highest economic growth rate in the world.

'The Northeast Asia Economic Zone'

An economic zone involving countries bordering the Japan Sea – Japan, South and North Korea, Northeast China, and Far East Russia – is emerging in Northeast Asia. It has great potential because of the endowment of natural resources and economic complementarity among potential members. As in other economic zones in Asia, countries in the Northeast Asia Economic Zone are seeking to promote cooperation and economic development through international trade and investment. The development of Far East Russia would require funds and technology from Japan and Korea, and labour from Northern China and North Korea. To cope with rising production costs at home, South Korea has shown interest in extending its economic frontier to neighbouring Chinese provinces and North Korea.

There has been a marked improvement in the relations among countries surrounding the Japan Sea since 1989, including the normalization of Sino-Soviet relations, and the establishment of diplomatic links between the Soviet Union and South Korea. A number of problems, including the territorial dispute between Russia and Japan over four of the northern islands and the antagonism between North and South Korea, nevertheless, remain to be solved before economic cooperation can yield real benefits.

Among the various moves towards economic cooperation by the countries surrounding the Japan Sea, the following four seem to be the most promising: (1) Japanese investment in Far East Russia, (2) economic exchanges between South Korea and China, (3) the Tumen River Development Project, and (4) South Korean investment in North Korea.

First, the natural resources of Far East Russia are extremely attractive to Japan. In the past economic exchanges between Japan and Far East Russia were seriously hindered by political and diplomatic hurdles. However, economic cooperation has expanded since the introduction of perestroika under the former Soviet Union, and in particular the dissolution of the Soviet Union in 1991. So far, Japanese investment in Far East Russia has been concentrated in the processing of marine products and in activities relating to agriculture and forestry. The potential of petroleum and natural gas development in Sakhalin remains untapped. Japanese companies will remain reluctant to expand their commitments in Far East Russia until political and economic stability is restored and a legal framework protecting foreign investors is in place. More support from the Japanese government would be forthcoming if the dispute over the sovereignty of the northern islands comes to be settled.

Second, economic exchanges across the Yellow Sea between South Korea and China have spawned the concept of the 'Yellow Sea Economic Zone'. Following Hong Kong and Taiwan's examples, South Korea is expanding its economic exchanges with China. The establishment of diplomatic relations in August 1992 cleared the last hurdle restricting trade and investment between the two countries.

Third, a major development project in the Tumen Delta area bordering North Korea, China and Russia is in progress under the auspices of the UN Development Program. South Korea and Japan have shown interest in participating in the project. However, the total investment needed is estimated to reach $30 billion, and the funding sources for the project have yet to be found. In addition, the Russian and Chinese governments are more committed to the development of Vladivostok and Hunchun within their own border than the Tumen River Project as a whole.

Fourth, progress has also been made in bilateral economic cooperation between South and North Korea. North Korea is negotiating with South Korea to establish an industrial park in the form of a joint venture in Nampo, located west of Pyongyang, the capital of North Korea. In the future, development projects similar to China's special economic zones may be launched along the 38th parallel demilitarized zone now separating the North from the South. Economic integration may serve as a catalyst for political integration between the North and the South. The experience of German unification suggests that the cost of an outright 'acquisition' of the North would be too high for the South to bear. A more probable scenario is that relations between the North and South will follow the China-Taiwan model, with freer trade and investment flows but limited labour mobility.

'The Indochina Economic Zone'

Thailand has been actively strengthening economic links with its neighbours in Indochina. Vietnam, Laos and Cambodia are well-endowed with petroleum, coal and other mineral resources needed for the industrialization of Thailand. In the long term, Thailand is also eyeing the region as an export market. Indochina suffered economic stagnation during the Vietnam War and the civil war in Cambodia. By promoting economic development in Indochina, Thailand hopes to maintain political stability in the region.

On the other hand, to take advantage of the dynamism in the Asia-Pacific region, Vietnam, Laos and Cambodia have shifted to more outward-looking development strategies. To strengthen economic links with its neighbours, Vietnam has expressed interest in joining ASEAN. The ASEAN countries have also softened their stance against Vietnam.

A number of problems remain to be solved before Indochina can grow into an economic zone comparable with that of South China. First, the fear of being dominated by Thailand has prompted Vietnam to strengthen its ties with other countries: in addition to the ASEAN countries, it is seeking investment from Japan, Taiwan, and Hong Kong. Indeed, Hong Kong is now challenging Bangkok as the gateway to Vietnam. Second, the socialist countries in Indochina have become more cautious in conserving their natural resources, which so far have been their major sources of foreign earnings. Third, economic cooperation has centred on bilateral relations between Thailand and the socialist countries. Further progress, including the development of the Mekong Delta, will require coordinated efforts among all participating countries. To achieve this end, Japan's prime minister Kiichi Miyazawa proposed to set up a 'Forum for Comprehensive Development in Indochina' during his trip to the ASEAN countries in January 1993.

Strengthening multilateral cooperation

As seen above, regional cooperation in Asia so far has been achieved mainly by the initiative of the private sector. Regional economic integration with coordination among governments in Asia has lagged far behind that in Europe and North America. Following Balassa (1961), regional economic integration can be classified into four stages – free trade area, custom union, common market and economic union – according to the extent to which members grant preferences to one another and coordinate policies among themselves.[7] Judged by this classification, regional economic integration in Asia has not even reached the first stage. Recently, however, multilateral economic cooperation at the government level is also gaining momentum (Figure 7.7).

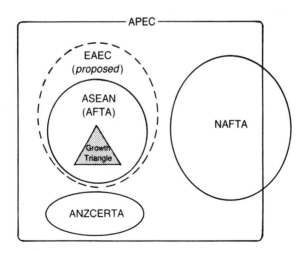

Figure 7.7 Multilateral economic cooperation in the Pacific region
Source: NRI.

133

The Association of Southeast Asian Nations (ASEAN) has remained the symbol of regional economic cooperation. ASEAN was established in 1967 between Indonesia, Malaysia, Philippines, Singapore and Thailand to foster regional economic and political cooperation. Brunei became the sixth member in 1984.

Until now, ASEAN has played an important role in political cooperation, but has yet to achieve significant results in the sphere of economic cooperation. The strengthening of regional cooperation is necessary, however, to cope with the rising tide of regionalism and to halt the shift of direct investment from the ASEAN countries to the new competitors such as China, Latin America and East European countries.

A major barrier to economic cooperation has been the relatively low degree of complementarity in economic structures among ASEAN members. This can be solved by extending membership to countries at different stages of economic development. Proposals along this line range from extending membership of ASEAN to the socialist countries in Indochina (Greater ASEAN) to promoting economic cooperation among all countries along the Western Pacific Rim, such as the East Asian Economic Caucus (EAEC) proposed by Malaysian Prime Minister Mahathir. The EAEC aims to exploit complementarity through economic cooperation by coupling those countries at a low stage of development, such as China and the three Indochinese countries, including Vietnam, with the economically-advanced countries, such as Japan and the NIEs. The EAEC, however, does not include countries on the other side of the Pacific as its potential members. This has prompted the United States to criticize the proposal as counterproductive and racist. In the absence of US support, Japan hesitates to take the lead in realizing this idea.

To enhance its attractiveness to foreign investors, ASEAN has decided to establish an ASEAN Free Trade Area (AFTA) over 15 years starting from 1993. The AFTA will cover trade in manufactured goods and processed agricultural products. A Common Effective Preferential Tariff (CEPT) scheme will be established and this will lead to a progressive reduction of tariffs to a 0–5 per cent level by 2008. By liberalizing trade in the area, AFTA should encourage horizontal division of labour in industrial goods, and boost the attractiveness of the ASEAN countries as a destination for direct investment.

ASEAN's restrictive requirement that all activities must benefit all member countries has also hindered economic cooperation among the ASEAN countries. To circumvent this, attempts have been made to seek cooperation among a smaller number of members outside the ASEAN framework (the six minus X formula), including the Growth Triangle between Singapore, Malaysia, and Indonesia, advocated by Singapore's Prime Minister Goh Chok Tong.[8]

The Growth Triangle concept calls for joint effort to develop Malaysia's Johor and Indonesia's Riau Province embracing Batam Island into manufacturing bases. Singapore will play a leading role by providing the infrastructure, management know-how, as well as other supporting services. Investors can optimize factor utilization by setting up their regional headquarters in Singapore, and locate different manufacturing processes in the three areas according to the land and labour requirements.

The Growth Triangle should mark the first step in further economic cooperation among Singapore, Indonesia and Malaysia. In the future, it may develop into a large economic zone that also includes the rest of Malaysia and Indonesia. Singapore will play the role of business service centre for this 'Maritime Southeast Asia Economic Zone', the same role Hong Kong is now playing for the South China Economic Zone. The Growth Triangle may be a model for other intra-ASEAN economic cooperation (such as the Northern Triangle encompassing neighbouring provinces in Malaysia, Indonesia and Thailand) to follow.

Meanwhile, Asia-Pacific Economic Cooperation (APEC) is emerging as the dominant force of economic cooperation in the Asia-Pacific region. Its members now include all the major players on both sides of the Pacific – the United States, Canada, Japan, NIEs, ASEAN, China, Australia and New Zealand. Since the first ministerial meeting in 1989, APEC's role has centred on the promotion of dialogue and cooperative sectoral projects to deal with the major problems affecting the region's economy. At the November 1991 conference in Seoul, APEC issued a declaration stating that it should be the duty of the group to serve as a model for open regional cooperation, and that it should strive to eliminate barriers to trade and investment among members, in conformity with the principles of GATT. At the September 1992 conference in Bangkok, it was decided to locate the secretariat in Singapore. These decisions represent the first steps in creating a free trade area encompassing countries on both sides of the Pacific Ocean. With the full support of both developed and developing countries in the region, APEC also has the potential to develop into a Pacific version of OECD.

APPENDIX: EXPANSION OF NEW FRONTIERS AND THE DUTCH DISEASE

The model discussed in the text can be extended to examine the Hong Kong version of the Dutch disease by introducing a non-tradable sector to the investing country.[9]

Consider three sectors: a non-tradable sector in Country A, a tradable sector in Country A and a tradable sector in Country B. The last two sectors are assumed to produce an identical good with an identical production function. Labour is assumed to be mobile between the non-tradable and tradable sectors in Country A (but not across national borders). Capital is assumed to be mobile only between the two sectors in country A initially, but among all three sectors when restrictions on capital flows are relaxed.

The impact on Country A of a relaxation of restrictions on capital flows can be analysed with reference to Figure 7.8. The initial equilibrium can be illustrated by the production possibility curve NT, which shows the combination of tradable and non-tradable goods attainable given the endowment of labour and capital (both assumed to be mobile between the two sectors). Assuming that income equals consumption, NT can also be interpreted as the consumption possibility curve. Initial equilibrium is at point E where the production possibility

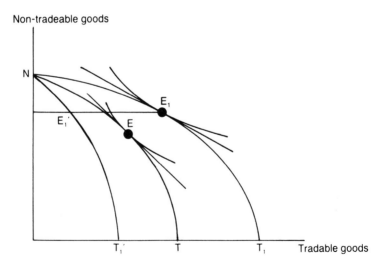

Figure 7.8 Expansion of new frontiers and macroeconomic performance
Source: NRI.

curve is tangential to the highest attainable social indifference curve. The initial price of the non-tradable sector (relative to that of the tradable) is given by the slope of the common tangent to the two curves at E.

The relaxation of restrictions on capital flows leads to a relocation of the mobile factors among the three different sectors, and divergence between the production possibility curve and the consumption possibility curve. Reflecting the shift of capital from Country A to Country B, the production possibility curve shrinks to NT_1'. On the other hand, the consumption possibility curve shifts outward to NT_1. Both the expansion of the consumption possibility curve and contraction of the production possibility are biased towards the tradable good sector.

The new equilibrium is reached at E_1, where the new consumption possibility curve is tangential to the highest social indifference curve. So long as the non-tradable good is a normal good (that is, the demand for it rises with increase in income), E_1 lies above E. Since the expansion of the consumption possibility curve is biased toward the tradable sector, the price of the non-tradable goods relative to that of the tradable good (given by the common tangent at E_1) must be higher than at E. Domestic production is at E_1', with higher production of the non-tradable good and lower production of the tradable good (de-industrialization). The difference between GNP and GDP, measured in terms of the tradable good, is given by the distance between E_1' and E_1.

Given export prices and import prices in terms of foreign currencies in international markets (the small country assumption), the change in the relative price between the non-tradable good and the tradable good can take the form of an inflation in the non-tradable sector, an appreciation of the exchange rate, or a combination of the two. In countries with fixed exchange rates, such as Hong Kong, expansion of new frontiers has led to chronic inflation. In the case of Taiwan, to curb inflation the government has allowed the local currency to appreciate.

Chronic inflation in Hong Hong has thus largely reflected the economic boom in southern China. For Hong Kong companies, southern China is like a newly-founded gold mine. A large part of the profits earned there is spent in Hong Kong. Rising demand, particularly in the service sector, has boosted inflation. This phenomenon shares some similarity with the hyper-inflation in Spain in the sixteenth century resulting from the influx of gold from the New World.

Recently, the linked exchange-rate system has been (incorrectly) blamed for the chronic inflation in Hong Kong. Proposals to suppress

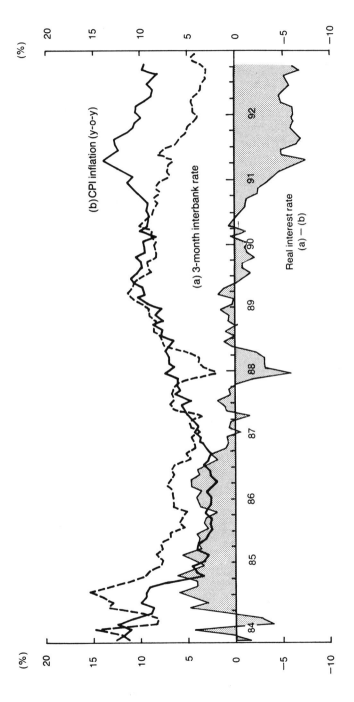

Figure 7.9 Inflation and interest rates in Hong Kong

Source: Compiled by NRI based on Hong Kong Census and Statistics Department, *Hong Kong Monthly Digest of Statistics.*

inflation range from revaluing the Hong Kong dollar against the US dollar, to pegging to a basket of currencies, and to allowing the Hong Kong dollar to float freely. Since inflation in Hong Kong is more structural than cyclical, the effect of a once-and-for-all revaluation can only be temporary (be it under the current dollar-linked system or a basket-peg system). Curbing inflation would require revaluing the local currency frequently, adopting a crawling peg system, or allowing the Hong Kong dollar to float freely. In view of the absence of a central bank (capable of controlling the money supply) and uncertainty facing Hong Kong during the transition to Chinese rule, any changes in the current system would only invite speculation on the Hong Kong dollar, which in turn would have adverse effect on the stability of the economy. The authorities are likely to maintain the current system, while paying the cost of high inflation.

Meanwhile, under the dollar peg system, interest rates in Hong Kong have followed very closely trends in the United States, reflecting arbitration between the two markets. The 3-month interbank rate in Kong Kong, for example, has followed the downward trend in US 3-month TB rate since 1989. Coupled with high inflation, real interest rates (nominal interest rates minus inflation) have stayed at negative levels since mid-1990 (Figure 7.9). The fall in real interest rates has been a major factor supporting stock prices and property prices. So long as southern China continues to grow at a rapid pace and interest rates in the United States remain low, the coexistence of high inflation and negative real interest rates will persist.

8

THE ASIAN ECONOMIES IN THE 1990s

INTRODUCTION[1]

In this chapter, we present our medium-term outlook for the Asian economies. In light of the growing uncertainties facing these countries, we have drawn up three scenarios, taking into consideration the possibility of sluggish economic growth in the world economy and political instability within the region. The first part of this chapter discusses the preconditions for maintaining high economic growth, while the second part presents the three scenarios. In addition, a check-list of the main points to note for each Asian country in the 1990s is included in the Appendix at the end of this chapter.

THE PRECONDITIONS FOR MAINTAINING HIGH GROWTH

Economic performance of the Asian countries in the 1990s will depend on the pace of world economic growth as well as their ability to maintain political stability and to solve structural problems in their economies.

Stable growth of the global economy

The growth prospects of the world economy remain mixed. Several factors are inhibiting the growth rate of developed nations, including the aging of their populations, slower growth of their work forces, and rising environmental and energy costs. Yet, hopes for stronger economic growth are pinned on the unification of the EC and rapid growth in Asia, as well as the cuts in military spending (the so-called peace dividend). Accounting for all these factors, in our baseline scenario we assume that global economic growth averages 2.8 per cent a year in the 1990s, matching that of the 1980s.

Nevertheless, factors that may drag down world economic growth also need to be taken into consideration. These down-side risks include a prolonged recession in the United States resulting from a failure to restructure its economy, the rise of protectionism, shortage of global savings and high interest rates, financial instability, skyrocketing oil prices, and escalating environmental problems. Therefore, we have also formulated an alternative scenario of the Asian economies based on the premise that the world economy grows at an annual rate of 1.8 per cent in the 1990s.

Concerns are growing that the rising tide of regionalism, as exemplified by EC and NAFTA, may lead to a disintegration of the world economy into trade blocs. We believe that open regionalism will contribute to the revitalization of the global economy and to rebuilding a free-trade system. Considering the recent intensification of trade friction and the difficulties of the GATT Uruguay Round negotiations, however, a possibility exists that regionalism will take the form of closed blocs. Should this happen, the highly-integrated world economy would suffer a devastating blow from stagnating trade and investment.

Political stability in the region

During the 1980s, a virtuous cycle of economic development and political stability took hold in Asia. The presence of the United States also acted as a stabilizing force in the region. Generally speaking, we expect these conditions to prevail in the 1990s also.

The balance maintained by the US-Soviet confrontation has crumbled now that the Cold War is over. In Asia, regional disputes due to ethnic, territorial, and other problems pose potential threats to stability. We must also be aware of the risk of political uncertainty within individual countries, socialist countries in particular. In some instances, the impact may not be limited to one country, but may have repercussions in neighbouring countries as well.

In contrast to the former Soviet Union and to the countries of the Eastern bloc, Asia's socialist countries are holding firm to authoritarian political regimes. In China and Vietnam, however, economic liberaliz-ation and the expansion of the market economy continue to make headway. Tension between political systems and changing economic reality may arise in the future. At the same time, political demands for autonomy from ethnic minorities in China may increase, and unification may occur on the Korean Peninsula.

There is also the risk of political instability arising from the transition of power to a new generation of leaders. Both China's Deng Xiaoping and Indonesia's Suharto have driven economic development with exceptionally strong leadership. Domestic turmoil may arise when they leave the political scene. A large outflow of refugees or violence against overseas Chinese could shake the entire Asian economy. In particular, a failure of economic reform in China would cast a shadow over Hong Kong, which is becoming the 'capital' of southern China.

Territorial problems could flare up once again in the South China Sea where large reserves of oil have been confirmed, and along the Sino-Vietnamese border. The countries concerned have begun to establish a cooperative system for resource development, however, so the territorial disputes may not materialize.

Domestic structural problems

In addition to the stable growth of the global economy and political stability within the region, several structural problems need to be solved to sustain the dynamism of the Asian economy in the 1990s.

The first problem to cope with is the need to upgrade the industrial structure so that the relocation of labour-intensive industries to lower-income countries does not lead to a hollowing-out of industry. It has become very common for Asian companies to move operations in industries that have lost competitiveness to another country with lower wages and other advantages. The hollowing-out of industry will proceed in the investing country unless the gain in growing industries more than compensates for the loss arising from the relocation of declining industries abroad. To prevent this the governments of the Asian countries are implementing policies for upgrading the industrial structure by transfer of technology from advanced countries and by improving productivity through investing in research and development. To prepare for the increased unemployment with the relocation of industries overseas, policies will be needed to ensure the smooth transition to new jobs, including the provision of unemployment assistance and vocational training.

The second problem is the need to strengthen the industrial base. The infrastructure in the Asian countries has been rendered inadequate by the sharp increase in direct investment that has made rapid growth possible. Most of these countries have ambitious plans to improve infrastructure in the 1990s. On the top of the list are Hong Kong's new airport and Taiwan's mega-projects related to its Six-year Development Plan. Korea will carry out major port development and transportation projects, including the development of the west coast region and the high-speed rail line linking Seoul and Pusan. In Indonesia, the construction of power-generating and communications networks has gotten under way. When these kinds of infrastructure development are delayed, private investment and the inflow of foreign direct investment will stagnate, with adverse effects on economic growth.

The third problem is the need to solve labour problems. As the demand for democracy grows in the NIEs, including Korea and Taiwan, workers have sought improvement in the standard of living through large wage increases. In some industries production costs have climbed and competitiveness has suffered from labour disputes and drastic wage increases. This hastens the hollowing-out of industry. To prevent this, the rate of increase of real wages must be held within the rate of increase of productivity. To cope with labour shortages, restrictions on the introduction of foreign labour will be widely relaxed. In addition, there is a chronic shortage of middle-management personnel and technicians in Asian countries, so higher education and vocational training must be strengthened.

The fourth problem is the need to correct income disparity. The fruits of economic growth are not always distributed equitably, and expanding income disparity among regions and ethnic groups may spark political and social unrest. In China, for example, per capita GNP has surpassed $1000 in some coastal cities, but remains below $250 in the inland provinces. In the ASEAN countries, overseas Chinese, who compose less than 10 per cent of the population, have dominated economic activities.

The fifth problem is the need to resolve trade friction. During the 1980s, the trade friction between the two sides of the Pacific spread from Japanese-US disputes to NIEs-US disputes and further to Chinese-US disputes. At the same time, growing intra-regional trade has been accompanied by widening bilateral trade gaps among the Asian countries themselves. Since large-scale direct investment is only a recent phenomenon, investing countries continue to expand exports of capital goods while their imports of goods produced in their overseas subsidiaries is still low. That is why Japan's trade surplus with the NIEs and the ASEAN countries continues to grow. In Korea and Taiwan in particular, the widening trade deficits with Japan, together with demands for technology transfer are becoming political problems. In the

ASEAN countries, current account deficits are also growing. Their combined trade balances with Japan, which had been in surplus, have recently turned into a deficit. To resolve these problems, the Asian countries' export markets must be further diversified, and Japan should open its market further to absorb more Asian exports.

THREE SCENARIOS FOR THE 1990s

Based on recent trends and potential problems discussed above, in this section, we project the performance of the Asian economies up to the year 2000. In addition to a baseline case based on the assumption of stable growth of the global economy and political stability in the region, two alternative scenario are presented. One is based on sluggish global economic growth and rising protectionism, and the other is based on political instability in the region (Figure 8.1).

The average rate of growth in Asia for the decade of the 1990s in the baseline scenario is projected at 7.7 per cent (probability: 55 per cent). In the sluggish global economic growth scenario, it is projected at 6.5 per cent (probability: 30 per cent), and in the political instability scenario, it is projected at 6.6 per cent (probability: 15 per cent). The expected growth rate considering the probability of the three scenarios is 7.1 per cent (Table 8.1).

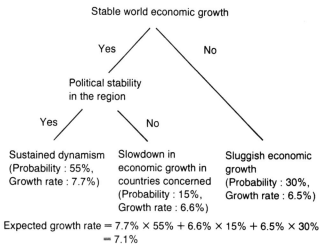

Figure 8.1 Three scenarios for the 1990s
Source: NRI.

Table 8.1 Economic growth rates of the Asian countries into the 1990s

	1970s	1980s	1990s			
			first half	*second half*	*Base case*	*Expected value*
NIEs	8.7	8.5	7.4	9.6	7.2	6.6
Korea	7.7	9.6	8.4	10.8	7.7	7.1
Taiwan	9.7	8.0	7.1	8.9	7.0	6.5
Hong Kong	9.3	6.7	5.6	7.9	6.2	5.5
Singapore	9.1	7.1	6.2	8.0	6.1	5.8
ASEAN	7.3	5.8	4.3	7.3	6.6	6.3
Indonesia	8.0	5.5	4.7	6.3	6.5	6.3
Malaysia	7.8	5.9	5.1	6.8	7.2	6.9
Philippines	6.3	1.8	−1.0	4.6	3.7	3.6
Thailand	6.8	7.7	5.6	9.9	8.0	7.4
China	5.8	8.9	10.2	7.7	9.1	8.5
NIEs + ASEAN + China	7.5	8.0	7.4	8.5	7.7	7.1
World	3.6	2.8	2.5	3.2	2.8	2.5

Note: Expected values are calculated as the weighted average of the baseline scenario and two alternative scenarios. Scenarios for individual countries also take into consideration factors specific to them, and therefore do not necessarily correspond to those for the region as a whole.
Source: IMF, *International Financial Statistics*, official statistics and NRI forecasts.

The baseline scenario – dynamism continues

In this scenario, the dynamism of the region is projected to continue. Assuming stable growth of the global economy (global economic growth rate in the 1990s averaging 2.8 per cent annually) and political stability in the region (the absence of wars or internal disorder), the rate of growth for the Asian region will reach 7.7 per cent.

Stable growth of the global economy will not only support exports and investment in the Asian countries but also promote structural adjustment and boost their medium-term growth rates. The Asia-Pacific region will remain the most dynamic part of the world economy, and its new frontiers will further expand with the entry of the socialist countries. In addition to the South China Economic Zone, other economic zones, including the Northeast Asia Economic Zone, the Yellow Sea Economic Zone, the Indochina Economic Zone, and the

Growth Triangle, will post impressive gains. The areas on the Western Pacific Rim may well develop into one large economic zone.

Economic development in the Asia-Pacific region is entering a new phase. The Asian NIEs are preparing to reach advanced-country status, while the ASEAN countries and China are getting ready to join the ranks of newly-industrializing nations. Based on the experience of Japan and the NIEs, the growth rate of the NIEs should decline in the 1990s, while that of the ASEAN countries should rise. As a result, the traditional pattern of economic growth in Asia characterized by high growth rates in countries in the north and low growth rates in countries in the south should break down and economic growth rates of the two regions are expected to converge in the medium term.

In the Asian NIEs, stable global economic growth will work as a factor supporting economic growth. These countries will continue to diversify from the US market and trade more with countries in Asia. Still they will have to rely more on domestic demand than on net exports as the engine of economic growth. As democratization gathers pace, the priority of government economic policy should shift from economic growth to improving the quality of life. More attention will be paid to the distribution of income, social welfare and environment protection. Turning to the supply side, the growth rate of the working population is projected to decline. There will also be a shift from investment in plant and equipment, which is directly linked to production, to investment in social capital. This will lead to a slowdown in productivity growth. To eliminate labour shortages, foreign workers have to be imported to support activity in the construction and service sectors, while corporations must accelerate the shift overseas of labour-intensive manufacturing industries.

Investment from the Asian NIEs will spread from the ASEAN countries and southern China to the other coastal regions of China, Vietnam, and North Korea. The relationship between North and South Korea will, like that between Taiwan and China, make progress based on economic exchanges. Taken together, the Asian NIEs' economic growth rate should reach 7.2 per cent a year in the 1990s.

Hong Kong's sovereignty is due to revert to China in 1997, as stipulated by the 1984 Sino-British agreement. The success of China's economic reform and open-door policy, as well as the vitality of the South China Economic Zone will enhance Hong Kong's role as the gateway to China, and contribute to its stability and prosperity. China has made the political pledge of autonomy and the economic promise of 'one country, two systems' to Hong Kong. China maintains that Hong

Kong will keep the existing capitalist system and way of life for 50 years, without switching to a socialist system. If this can be accomplished with few hitches, the chances for the unification of China and Taiwan will improve.

In the ASEAN countries, the inflow of direct investment has boosted economic growth and promoted industrialization by relaxing bottlenecks in the availability of technology and domestic savings. Progress in regional integration, by promoting the division of labour according to comparative advantage, will enhance the attractiveness of ASEAN as a destination for foreign direct investment. The emergence of the NIEs as major investors in the region, and the relaxation of regulations governing foreign investment by the recipient countries, will also help to sustain the inflow of direct investment. As a result, a virtuous circle in which investment increases exports and exports induce further investment will continue to hold, as in the case of the Asian NIEs during the 1960s. With this as a backdrop, the average annual economic growth of four ASEAN countries – Indonesia, Malaysia, the Philippines, and Thailand – as a group will accelerate from 5.8 per cent in the 1980s to 6.6 per cent in the 1990s. The current account balances of the ASEAN countries, which have worsened over the past few years, are expected to improve as exports expand.

The dynamism of the Asian economy is spreading to the socialist countries of the region. In China, the policies of economic reform and liberalization are expected to continue and a market economy will be firmly established by 2000. Average economic growth should reach 9.1 per cent a year in the 1990s, the highest in the world. Much success has been achieved in reforming the agricultural sector, but the reform of the industrial sector in general, and state-owned enterprises in particular, will be the most important policy issue in the 1990s. Success in reforming the state-owned enterprises will trigger a new vitality in the Chinese economy. In Vietnam, the resumption of official development aid and the influx of foreign investment will transform the country from a closed economy to an active member in the regional economy. North Korea's opening to the outside world will also speed up economic exchange with neighbouring countries, including South Korea. Progress in economic development, together with the passing away of the old guard, should pave the way for political reform in the socialist countries.

With this high growth as a backdrop, Asia's growing importance in the world economy has become an inevitable trend. The share of the global economy accounted for by the Asian NIEs, ASEAN, and China as a group is forecast to rise from 5 per cent in 1990 to 8.2 per cent in

2000 in terms of GNP, and from 12.3 per cent to 17.2 per cent in terms of trade value. With the Asian economy expected to grow at a rate 2.5 times that of the global average, the share of intra-regional trade among Japan, the Asian NIEs, ASEAN, and China will rise from 40 per cent to more than 50 per cent by 2000. Asia will absorb over 40 per cent of total Japanese exports and the Asian NIEs alone will replace the United States as Japan's largest export market.

Today, most intra-regional trade is in capital and intermediate goods. As incomes rise, however, trade in consumer goods will grow in importance. Over the medium-term, the role of Asia for Japanese corporations will gradually shift from being a site for offshore production to a market for finished products. Asian exports to Japan are also expected to show steady growth, primarily in manufactured goods. The configuration of horizontal division of labour in Asia will gradually shift from specialization by production processes to specialization by finished manufactured goods.

Alternative scenario A – sluggish world economic growth

Based on the premise of sluggish global economic growth (with an annual global economic growth rate of 1.8 per cent in the 1990s) and intensified trade friction, Asian exports will slow down and economic growth will be held to an annual rate of 6.5 per cent.

If the cause of the global economic slump is a protracted economic slowdown in the US economy resulting from the failure to restructure the economy, we anticipate a resurgence of protectionism and the intensification of trade friction with the United States. In addition to the problem of China's most-favoured-nation status, the problem of Thailand and Malaysia graduating from the General System of Preferences (GSP) will surface, dealing a blow to the export-driven growth of the Asian countries.

To deal with these problems, Asian countries will have to diversify their export markets further and rely more on growth driven by domestic demand. While this will result in slower export growth, the share of intra-regional trade would rise above that of the baseline scenario. A sluggish global economy would not only restrain exports from Asian countries, but would also dampen the inflow of foreign capital and domestic investment, with a negative effect on the expansion of production capacity over the medium term.

If the cause of the global economic slump is soaring oil prices caused by the outbreak of war in the Middle East, Asian oil-producing nations would benefit slightly. For the Asia-Pacific region as a whole, however, long-term growth would be curbed by such factors as a deterioration in the terms of trade accompanying rising costs of imports, as well as a slump in exports to the markets of advanced countries.

If the reason for the global economic slump is high interest rates caused by rising demand for funds in Eastern Europe and the former Soviet Union, this will squeeze the funds available to Asia. The inflow of direct investment will slow, and investment in infrastructure will be retarded. The burden of debt repayment will increase for heavily-indebted countries such as the Philippines and Indonesia, leading unavoidably to a policy of austerity.

Alternative scenario B – political instability in Asia

Based on the premises of stable global economic growth (with an average annual global economic growth rate of 2.8 per cent) and political instability in the region caused by frequent regional disputes and civil disturbances, Asia's investment climate will worsen with growth falling to 6.6 per cent.

Of the above-mentioned political instability, turmoil in China in particular, would be the harshest blow to the regional economy. Pushing reforms too fast and too far may lead to economic dislocation. This would include overheated domestic demand caused by rising inflation, increases in unemployment accompanying the bankruptcies of inefficient state-owned enterprises, and the expansion of income disparities. An unstable China would obstruct the economic integration of the economies of Hong Kong, Taiwan and southern China. In Hong Kong, there would be a drastic increase in the number of emigrants and capital outflows before its reversion to China in 1997.

A chaotic Chinese economy also would cast a shadow over the unification of China and Taiwan. The Kuomintang government in Taiwan would inevitably shift from its current policy of a gradual approach to unification to a gradual approach to independence. Taiwan's economy would also be affected by Chinese political instability. Direct investment and technological transfer from overseas would stagnate, and industrial development would come to a standstill.

For risks involving Asia's socialist countries, the trends in North Korea cannot be overlooked. If the current political system in the country breaks down, North-South unification could probably be realized through the absorption of the North by the South. The experience of Germany, however, shows that unification costs can be immense, putting a huge burden on the Korean economy.

The risks involving temporary political instability accompanying the transition of political power in Indonesia, Malaysia, the Philippines, and other Asian countries cannot be ignored. Compared to turmoil in the socialist countries, however, the effects would be confined to the domestic economies.

APPENDIX: A CHECKLIST FOR INDIVIDUAL COUNTRIES IN THE 1990s

South Korea

Key points to note

Relations with the North and unification.
Liberalization and opening of capital markets.
Upgrading of industry.
Correction of regional imbalances.
Infrastructure development.

Factors favouring economic development

Rising income levels and growing domestic demand.
High educational levels.
Superior bureaucracy.
Economic exchange with China and North Korea.

Factors inhibiting economic development

High inflation.
Weak technology base.
Inadequate infrastructure.
Inefficient industrial organization.
North Korea's political instability.

Taiwan

Key points to note

Relations with China.
The South China Economic Zone.

GATT membership.
Six-Year National Development Plan
Financial reform, including development of the bond market.

Factors favouring economic development

Abundant funds.
Strong domestic demand.
High educational levels.
Economic exchange with China.
Linkage with southern China.

Factors inhibiting economic development

Uncertainty over political relations with China.
Labour shortages.
Sluggish private investment.
Weak technology base.
Inadequate infrastructure.

Hong Kong

Key points to note

The return to China in 1997.
Economic integration with southern China.
Financial and trading centre for overseas Chinese.
New airport and related projects.
Direct expressway link with Guangdong Province.

Factors favoring economic development

Strategic location.
Economic reform and open-door policy in China.
Development of the South China Economic Zone.
Highly-developed infrastructure.

Factors inhibiting economic development

Inflation.
Brain drain.
Rising labour and land costs.

Singapore

Key points to note

Business centre for ASEAN.
Development of knowledge- and technology-intensive industries.
Growth of local business groups.
The Growth Triangle.

Factors favoring economic development

Highly-developed infrastructure.
Political stability.
High-quality labour.
Strategic location
ASEAN economic development.

Factors inhibiting economic development

Heavy dependence on foreign capital.
Rising labour and land costs.
Small domestic market.

Indonesia

Key points to note

Post-Suharto leadership.
Oil market conditions at home and abroad.
The Growth Triangle.
Major infrastructure projects.

Factors favouring economic development

Political stability.
Financial support from industrial countries.
Abundant natural resources and labour.
A large domestic market.

Factors inhibiting economic development

Inadequate infrastructure.
Economic disparities between ethnic groups.
Heavy debt burden.

Malaysia

Key points to note

Economic development emphasizing the private sector and markets.
The development of supporting industries.
Growth of local business groups.
The Growth Triangle.

Factors favouring economic development

Political stability.
Liberal policy towards foreign investment.
Proximity to Singapore.
Strengthening ties with other ASEAN countries.

Factors inhibiting economic development

Labour shortages
Inadequate infrastructure.
Underdeveloped supporting industry.
Heavy dependence on foreign capital.
Economic disparities between ethnic groups.

Philippines

Key points to note

Privatization of state-owned corporations.
Development of former American military bases (Clark, Subic).
Progress in land reform.

Factors favouring economic development

High-quality labour and low labour costs.

Good international relations.
Waning communist influence.

Factors inhibiting economic development

Poverty in countryside.
Political instability.
Heavy debt repayment burden.
Inconsistent government policies.
Fiscal deficits.
Inadequate infrastructure, particularly electricity generating capacity.

Thailand

Key points to note

Political democratization.
Expanding domestic markets.
The internationalization of financial markets.
Infrastructure development.
The Indochina Economic Zone.

Factors favouring economic development

Expanding exports of industrial manufactured goods.
Rising income levels.
Abundant natural resources and labour.
Rising economic exchange with Indochina.

Factors inhibiting economic development

Shortage of skilled-labour and inadequate infrastructure.
Insufficient supporting industry.
Worsening environment.
Income disparities.
Overcrowding in Bangkok.

China

Key points to note

The transition to a socialist market economy.
The post-Deng Xiaoping leadership.
Reform of state-owned enterprises and the financial system.
Infrastructure development.
The return of Hong Kong.

Factors favouring economic development

The acceleration of reform and open-door policy.
The replacement of central planning by the market mechanism.
Improving investment climate.
Vast domestic market.
Rising inflow of foreign direct investment, particularly from overseas Chinese.

Factors inhibiting economic development

Low productivity of state-owned enterprises.
Fiscal deficits.
Population problem.
Inflation.
Income disparities between coastal and inland regions.

Vietnam

Key points to note

Lifting of the US trade embargo.
Infrastructure development with Japanese ODA.
Establishing the institutional framework for promoting foreign investment.
Oil field development.

Factors favouring economic development

Abundance of oil and other natural resources.
High-quality labour and low labour costs.

An improving international environment.
Linkage with the South China Economic Zone.

Factors inhibiting economic development

US trade embargo.
Economic disparities between north and south.
Extreme shortage of funds.
Inflation and unemployment.
Underdeveloped infrastructure.

9

FORMATION OF A YEN BLOC

INTRODUCTION[1]

Interest in the possibility of forming a yen bloc between Japan and its Asian neighbours has increased in recent years against the background of growing Japanese economic and financial power, deepening economic interdependence between Japan and the Asian countries, and monetary integration in the EC. The traditional approach to this issue, along the lines of 'the internationalization of the yen', has a distinctive Japanese perspective. To deepen our understanding further, we also need to add a perspective of the Asian countries (NIEs and ASEAN), which are supposed to be potential members of the bloc.

Most people dismiss the idea of forming a yen bloc centring on Japan and encompassing the Asian countries as immature if not irrelevant. In most cases, arguments against a yen bloc are based on political considerations; most Asian countries would like to keep Japan at an arm's length because of the memory of Japanese occupation during the Second World War. However, the recent experience of monetary integration between Germany and France, two countries that fought each other in two world wars in this century alone, suggests that political barriers can be overcome. In the case of Asia, the political cost seems to be falling over time while the economic benefit seems to be rising. The idea of forming of a yen bloc will become mature when the economic benefit surpasses the political cost. Malaysia's proposal of forming an East Asian Economic Caucus, in which Japan is expected to play a leading role while the United States is excluded, suggests that a yen bloc is no longer an idea ahead of its time.

As an in-depth analysis of the political aspect of a yen bloc would be beyond the scope of this book, in what follows we limit ourselves to economic considerations. This chapter starts by reviewing evidence of the use of the yen as a regional currency. Four analytical approaches to a yen bloc are then identified. Finally, we conclude this chapter by drawing implications from our analysis in the previous chapters for the possibility of forming a yen bloc in the Asia-Pacific region.

THE USE OF THE YEN AS A REGIONAL CURRENCY

As Holloway (1990) notes, the term 'yen bloc' can mean two different things:

The broad definition. In this view, Japan becomes the centre of gravity of the West Pacific economy by virtue of its size – it comprises two-thirds of the region's annual output – and technological lead. As the region becomes increasingly integrated, more business activity enters the gravitational pull of Japan and its corporations. Trade and investment with the rest of the world continue to grow, but at a slower rate than within the region.

The narrower, monetary definition. The Japanese currency is used increasingly for regional trade and financial transactions, to the point where countries find it convenient to peg their currencies to the yen. The eventual result may be some form of monetary union, as is evolving in the EC, in which a common currency emerges.

In line with the narrower definition, a yen bloc is used here to refer to a grouping of countries among which the Japanese currency is widely used as an international (or a regional) currency, and where countries maintain stable exchange rates against the yen. As such, a yen bloc is analogous to such currency blocs as the former Sterling Area and the Economic and Monetary Union (EMU) now taking shape in the European Community. If the broader definition is used, there seems to be little room for argument; our analysis of growing interdependence among the Asian countries in previous chapters has provided overwhelming evidence that a yen bloc has already taken shape.[2]

Parallel to a domestic currency, an international currency performs the functions of a medium of exchange, unit of account and store of value. As a medium of exchange, it is used to settle international trade and financial transactions. As a unit of account, an international currency is used in invoicing international trade, denominating financial instruments, and expressing exchange-rate relations. As a store of value, it serves as an investment asset, including foreign exchange reserves of central banks. In addition, an international currency also acts as a peg for the currencies of smaller countries. The evidence of the use of the yen as an international currency is summarized in Figure 9.1.[3]

The US dollar has remained the dominant international currency in the Asia-Pacific region. As we have seen in Chapter 4, the dollar is still playing the role of an 'anchor' for the Asian currencies, although these countries no longer fix their exchange rates against it. At the same time, the dollar also dominates the yen in current transactions (trade in goods and services), financial transactions and foreign exchange reserves of central banks in the region. The yen is more often used than the dollar only as a currency denominating external debts of the Asian countries.

The bulk of the Asian countries' current account transactions continue to be denominated in dollars. In the case of South Korea, for example, current account receipts and payments denominated in dollars make up about 80 per cent of the total, compared with about 10 per

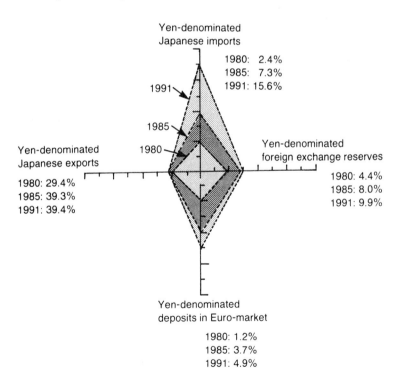

Yen-denominated
Japanese imports

1980: 2.4%
1985: 7.3%
1991: 15.6%

1991

1985

1980

Yen-denominated
Japanese exports

1980: 29.4%
1985: 39.3%
1991: 39.4%

Yen-denominated
foreign exchange reserves

1980: 4.4%
1985: 8.0%
1991: 9.9%

Yen-denominated
deposits in Euro-market

1980: 1.2%
1985: 3.7%
1991: 4.9%

Figure 9.1 Internationalization of the yen
Source: Japanese Ministry of Finance, IMF, BIS.

cent for transactions denominated in yen (Figure 9.2). The upward trend in the share of yen-denominated current account transactions seen in the first half of the 1980s has come to a halt in recent years. The bulk of yen-denominated current-account transactions involve trade with Japan; the use of the yen in trade with third countries is minimal.

Even in Japan itself, the dollar has maintained its position as the major invoicing currency in trade with Asian neighbours, although the share of yen-denominated trade has increased in recent years. In 1991 the proportion of exports to Southeast Asia denominated in yen reached 50.8 per cent, but that of imports was only 21.6 per cent. On the whole, there is a tendency for trade in standardized products (raw materials and fuels, and chemical goods, for example) to be denominated in dollars and differentiated products (motor vehicles, machinery, etc.) to be denominated in yen (Table 9.1). Starting from a very low base of 2 per cent, the proportion of Japan's imports from Southeast Asia denominated in yen has increased at a much faster pace than that for exports, reflecting the rising share of manufactured goods in Japanese imports from these countries.

The yen performs better as a regional currency denominating financial transactions. The proportion of external debts of the Asian countries denominated in yen has actually surpassed that denominated in dollars. The Thai government's external debt denominated in yen, for example, has exceeded that denominated in dollars since 1987 (Figure 9.3). This has been due more to the revaluation effect of the sharp

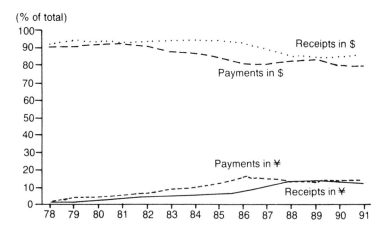

Figure 9.2 South Korea's current-account transaction by settlement currency
Source: *Economic Statistics Yearbook* and *Monthly Bulletin*, Bank of Korea.

Table 9.1 Currency denomination of Japan's trade by region and commodity

Exports, % of total

	Southeast Asia		USA		EC		All regions	
	¥	$	¥	$	¥	$	¥	$
Foodstuffs	42.5	55.7	23.6	76.3	64.8	22.7	41.2	55.6
Textile goods	28.5	71.0	19.5	80.1	60.4	9.3	32.5	63.0
Chemical goods	20.1	78.6	25.0	74.8	38.1	14.1	26.2	63.0
Non-metal mineral products	36.7	61.3	21.1	78.8	56.1	9.0	40.5	53.5
Metal goods	19.9	78.8	10.6	89.3	43.6	22.4	19.5	76.8
(Iron and steel)	10.9	88.6	0.9	99.1	16.2	44.2	9.4	87.7
Machinery	62.6	33.2	16.6	83.3	42.2	5.9	42.8	42.2
(Motor vehicles)	69.8	19.1	13.9	86.1	36.8	0.5	35.3	44.2
Total exports	50.8	45.9	16.5	83.4	42.0	6.8	39.4	46.8

Imports, % of total

	Southeast Asia		USA		EC		All regions	
	¥	$	¥	$	¥	$	¥	$
Foodstuffs	26.3	73.1	14.8	85.1	40.3	22.2	22.2	72.4
Raw materials and fuels	2.4	97.4	1.5	98.5	22.1	50.0	1.9	97.2
(Petroleum and petroleum products)	0.0	100.0	0.0	100.0	0.0	100.0	0.0	100.0
Manufactured goods	32.8	63.8	12.6	87.2	30.4	13.5	23.7	60.0
(Chemical goods)	28.0	69.8	15.1	84.6	58.5	12.3	32.5	51.7
(Machinery)	43.9	49.5	12.4	87.4	17.9	7.3	22.5	52.5
(Other manufactured goods)	29.0	68.5	11.6	88.1	26.9	21.5	21.9	66.9
Total imports	21.6	76.5	11.2	88.7	31.4	15.9	15.6	75.4

Source: Japanese Ministry of International Trade and Industry.

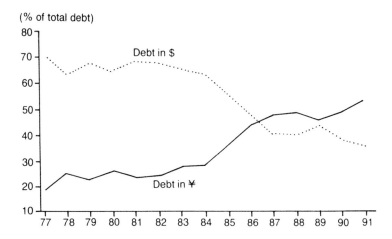

(% of total debt)

Figure 9.3 Thailand's government external debt classified by currency
Source: Bank of Thailand, *Monthly Bulletin*.

appreciation of the yen since 1985 than to a larger proportion of borrowing from Japan.

The proportion of the yen in the foreign exchange holdings of the Asian countries increased sharply in the first half of the 1980s, but this upward trend has come to a halt in recent years. At 17.5 per cent for selected Asian countries in 1989, it was substantially lower than that of the dollar (56.4 per cent) and only comparable to that of the Deutschmark (15.2 per cent).[4]

FOUR ANALYTIC APPROACHES TO A YEN BLOC

A yen bloc can be studied from four alternative (and complementary) approaches – (1) the internationalization of the yen, (2) the yen as an international currency, (3) optimum currency areas and (4) optimal pegs for developing countries – which offer, respectively, Japanese, global, regional and Asian perspectives. The first two approaches place more emphasis on the 'yen' aspect, while the latter two focus on the 'bloc' aspect of the issue.

Internationalization of the yen

The literature along the lines of 'the internationalization of the yen (*En no Kokusaika*)' can be extended to offer a *Japanese perspective* of a yen bloc. The focus is on the advantages and disadvantages for Japan of increasing the use of the yen as an international currency and its implications for domestic economic policy, including whether the internationalization of the yen should be promoted.

Until the early 1980s, the Japanese authorities were reluctant to internationalize the yen for fear that: (1) larger fluctuations in demand for the currency would destabilize the Japanese economy and make it difficult to conduct monetary policy; and (2) an increase in average demand for the currency would cause it to appreciate and hurt exports (Suzuki, 1989).

With Japan emerging as the world's largest creditor country in the second half of the 1980s, however, the Japanese authorities have changed their attitude. Since almost all of Japan's foreign assets are denominated in US dollars and therefore subject to the risk of exchange-rate fluctuations, it would be desirable for Japan to increase its proportion of yen-denominated assets. At the same time, the internationalization of the yen would help promote Tokyo as an international financial centre, bringing more business for Japan's banks and other financial institutions. In an attempt to enhance the attractiveness of yen holdings by non-residents, the authorities have speeded up the development of the Tokyo money market.

Studies along the lines of the internationalization of the yen have so far been formulated in the form of Japan versus the world. Indeed, in MOF (1992), the standard reference for the subject, there is no mention of the Asian countries at all. To be a useful tool for analysing the yen bloc, the advantages and disadvantages for Japan of forming a monetary union with its Asian neighbours need to be explicitly considered.

The yen as an international currency

Studies along the lines of 'the yen as an international currency' can be extended to offer a *global perspective* of the issue. The starting point is to examine the conditions for an international currency and to what extent the Japanese yen meets these conditions. Comparisons are usually made between the roles of the yen and other major key currencies (the dollar and the Deutschmark in particular) as international currencies.

As summarized in Tavlas and Ozeki (1991) and Frankel (1991b), the principal conditions for an international currency are: (1) a relatively low inflation rate in the issuing country, which contributes to a stable external value of the currency; and (2) deep, open and broad financial markets. Supplementary conditions include a country's share of world exports, the share of its exports comprising differentiated manufactured goods, and the extent of its trade with developing countries. These factors generally imply a growing role for the yen as an international currency.

When applied to a yen bloc, the analysis has been more descriptive than analytical. The focus has been on the use of the yen in the invoicing of trade in the Asia-Pacific region, denominating regional capital flows, and reserve holdings of the central banks of Asian countries. However, insufficient attention has been paid to the possibility of the yen becoming a currency to which the Asian currencies can be pegged. At the same time, the implications of increasing the use of the yen as an international currency for the international monetary system deserve further study.

Optimum currency areas

The theory of optimum currency areas, by studying which areas or countries should adopt (genuinely) fixed exchange rates among themselves, while allowing flexible rates in relation to the rest of the world, can provide a *regional perspective* (and a more direct approach) to a yen bloc. The traditional approach to the theory of optimum currency areas tries to single out a crucial economic characteristic which supposedly indicates where the lines between different blocs should be drawn.[5] The principal criteria determining the domain of an optimum currency area cited in the literature can be classified into five groups: (1) the extent of economic and financial integration; (2) similarity of economic structures; (3) similarity of policy objectives (notably preference between price stability and employment); (4) degree of policy integration; (5) presence of automatic market mechanisms, notably labour mobility and wage-price flexibility, that reduce the need to use the exchange rate as an instrument for redressing macroeconomic imbalances. A number of studies have attempted to determine the preconditions for a yen bloc by asking whether Asia is an optimum currency area.[6]

Drawing from the European experience, Holloway (1990) identifies a common tariff wall, the free movement of goods, services, labour and capital within a common market, and rough parity among members in their level of economic development as the major preconditions for the formation of a monetary union. Since these preconditions are not currently met in Asia, he concludes that the formation of a yen bloc is unrealistic at this stage. Suzuki (1989), however, views growing trade between Japan and the Asian countries (intra-industry trade in manufactured goods in particular) as a factor favourable to increasing the use of the yen as an international currency in Asia.

Park and Park (1990) are sceptical about the formation of a yen bloc between Japan and the Asian countries. Unfavourable factors cited include: (1) the still high dependence of the Asian countries on the US market; (2) Japan's limited capacity and willingness to absorb Asian imports; (3) the lead in Japanese technology and the high Japanese savings rate that necessitate frequent devaluations of the Asian currencies against the yen to prevent deterioration in their current accounts; (4) the unwillingness of the Asian countries to lose monetary autonomy and to tolerate a worsening of the inflation-unemployment trade-off; (5) the unlikeliness that a monetary union centring on the yen could narrow inflation differentials among members; and (6) the concern among Asian countries that monetary union could pave the way for political union.

The focus of the theory of optimum currency areas has been limited to relations within a given area. When applied to a situation of fluctuating exchange rates among different currency areas, more attention needs to be paid to the relations with the rest of the world.

Optimal pegs for developing countries

The literature on optimal pegs for developing countries (or small open economies) tries to evaluate the costs and benefits of pegging to some currency or basket of currencies (or participation in a monetary union) from the point of view of the self-interest of the particular region or country (see Chapter 4). It can provide an *Asian perspective* of a yen bloc when the developing countries refer to the Asian countries and the currency union uses the yen as the common currency.

While a number of criteria have been identified as important in determining the optimal peg, Kwan (1992) represents the first attempt in applying this approach to the analysis of a yen bloc. The conclusions of that paper are presented below.

AN ASIAN PERSPECTIVE OF A YEN BLOC

Choosing a currency to use in international transactions can be considered conceptually as a two-stage process. The first stage involves choosing an exchange-rate regime, which determines the relations of the domestic currency against foreign currencies. This decision is usually undertaken by the government, taking into consideration its policy objectives. The second stage involves the actual choice of which currency (currencies) to use by economic agents in denominating trade and financial instruments under the given exchange regime.[7] While the decision at the first stage usually involves macroeconomic objectives, that at the second stage is mainly based on microeconomic considerations involving balancing risks and returns (or costs). The advantages and disadvantages of joining a yen bloc for the Asian countries need therefore to be considered at both the macro and micro levels.

Macroeconomic considerations

The Asian countries have, up to now, focused on the bilateral rates between their local currencies and the dollar when formulating exchange-rate policy. However, they have experienced drastic changes in their regional composition of trade and inflows of foreign direct investment, and wide fluctuations in economic growth brought about by the global exchange-rate realignment since 1985. To adapt to the new international environment, the traditional exchange-rate policy of pegging loosely to the dollar may have to be amended, and more emphasis may have to be put on other major currencies, the Japanese yen in particular.

Our analysis in Chapter 4 suggests that, when the policy objective is to stabilize output, a country should peg its currency to a basket with large weights for competitors' currencies and small or even negative weights for major suppliers' currencies.[8] When applied to the Asian countries, the Asian NIEs (Korea and Taiwan in particular), which have export structures similar to that of Japan, may benefit by pegging to the yen (or by raising the weight of the yen in the reference basket of currencies when managing their exchange rates). The reverse may be true for primary commodity exporters that rely heavily on Japan for imports (the ASEAN countries, for example). Other things being equal, the Asian NIEs have more incentive than the ASEAN countries to peg their exchange rates to the yen.

The argument that the Asian countries should peg their currencies to the dollar because the United States is their largest export market can be challenged on two grounds. First, being the major market does not usually imply being a competitor, or an unimportant supplier, of the exporter country, so that the weight in the optimal basket of the currency of a trading partner does not need to be proportional to that country's share of the host country's exports.[9] Second, the share of Asian countries' exports to the United States has been declining rapidly since 1986 anyway, as we have seen in Chapter 6. This trend is expected to continue in the future in view of the need for the United States to reduce its trade deficit, and in its place, the share of intra-regional trade among Asian countries is expected to increase.

The current rapid pace of industrialization in the Asian countries is expected to continue, and this should favour a more important role for the yen in managing their exchange-rate policies. The Asian NIEs' commodity composition of exports will become increasingly similar to that of Japan, while the ASEAN countries' export composition will approach that of the Asian NIEs, as we have seen in Chapter 5. As a result, the benefits – in terms of output stability – for an Asian country of pegging its currency to the yen will increase. This is especially true when other Asian countries are also pegging their currencies to the yen.

Instead of forming a yen bloc, monetary integration in the Asia-Pacific region could also be achieved by pegging exchange rates of member countries to an 'Asian Currency Unit' or ACU, analogous to the ECU in the EC. The currency composition of the ECU is broadly in line with the relative economic power of the EC members, with the weight of the Deutschmark reaching 30.1 per cent (Table 9.2). If the same rule applies to the ACU, the Japanese yen should have a weight of over 50 per cent.

Microeconomic considerations

The volatility of the Asian currencies against the yen seems to be the major factor restraining the use of the yen as a regional currency, in contrast to the role the Deutschmark plays in the EC. Should the Asian countries shift from their current exchange-rate regimes of pegging loosely to the dollar to pegging to the yen (or raising substantially the weight of the yen in their current currency baskets), the cost-benefit analysis at the microeconomic level may favour more extensive use of the yen as a regional currency (other things being equal). More Asian importers and exporters would then prefer invoicing in the yen instead of the dollar; and borrowers and investors, including governments and central banks, would be more willing to hold a larger proportion of their portfolios in yen-denominated financial instruments.

By lowering the risk associated with exchange-rate fluctuations, pegging to the yen may also benefit the Asian countries by expanding their trade with, and capital inflows (foreign direct investment in

Table 9.2 Relative economic size and composition of common currency basket

		GDP or GNP (1991)		Exports + Imports (1991)		
	($ bil.)	Share (%)	Per capita ($)	($ bil.)	Share (%)	Weight in ECU (%)
Europe (ECU)						
Germany	1,554	25.0	24,361	793	28.1	30.1
France	1,192	19.2	21,024	449	15.9	19.0
Italy	1,134	18.3	19,637	352	12.5	10.2
United Kingdom	1,006	16.2	17,473	395	14.0	13.0
Spain	524	8.4	13,429	153	5.4	5.3
Netherlands	285	4.6	18,960	259	9.2	9.4
Belgium	197	3.2	19,980	238	8.4	7.6
Luxembourg	9	0.1	23,525			0.3
Denmark	131	2.1	25,500	68	2.4	2.5
Portugal	69	1.1	6,493	42	1.5	0.8
Greece	69	1.1	6,744	30	1.1	0.8
Ireland	43	0.7	12,321	45	1.6	1.1
EC Total	6,213	100.0	18,854	2,825	100.0	100.0

Asia						
Japan	3,363	79.3	27,105	552	39.9	–
NIEs	585	13.8	8,062	617	44.6	–
S. Korea	283	6.7	6,550	154	11.1	–
Taiwan	180	4.3	8,815	139	10.1	–
Hong Kong	82	1.9	14,155	199	14.4	–
Singapore	40	0.9	12,835	125	9.1	–
ASEAN	293	6.9	914	213	15.4	–
Indonesia	110	2.6	606	55	4.0	–
Malaysia	45	1.1	2,475	71	5.1	–
Philippines	45	1.1	716	21	1.5	–
Thailand	92	2.2	1,619	66	4.8	–
Japan + NIEs + ASEAN	4,240	100.0	8,203	1,382	100.0	–

Note: The weight of each currency in the ECU is determined by its physical amount in the ECU basket (composition) and current exchange rates. Figures in the table show the weights on 21 September 1989, after the recomposition of the basket.
Source: Compiled by NRI based on IMF, *International Financial Statistics*, OECD *Main Economic Indicators*, and official statistics of individual countries.

particular) from, Japan. This has become all the more important now that Japan has replaced the United States as the largest investor in Asia, and the United States alone can no longer play the role of locomotive for the Asian countries.[10]

Concluding remarks

Development of a yen bloc is still at an embryonic stage and research on it has lagged further behind. To deepen our understanding of the issue, the four approaches surveyed above need to be further developed and integrated to give a comprehensive and consistent 'general theory'. So far, studies have focused on the 'yen' aspect (from the Japanese and global perspectives) and insufficient attention has been paid to the 'bloc' aspect (from the regional and Asian perspectives) of the issue. By focusing on the latter aspect, our analysis should provide some essential components that have so far been missing for constructing such a theory.

NOTES

1 AN OVERVIEW

1 See, for example, Chen (1990).
2 The top ten container ports in the world in 1991 were: Singapore, Hong Kong, Kaohsiung, Rotterdam, Pusan, Kobe, Hamburg, Los Angeles, Keelung, New York (Source: Containerization Yearbook).
3 For a detailed study of the implications of Reaganomics on the US twin deficits, see Friedman (1988).

2 BALANCE-OF-PAYMENTS IMBALANCES AND EXCHANGE-RATE REALIGNMENT

1 This section is based on Kwan (1990a).
2 The balance of trade is defined to include both goods and services and transfer payments so that

   Balance of current account
      = Balance of trade + Balance of investment income.

3 The approach here follows Kindleberger (1968) and World Bank (1985).
4 For an explanation of the balance-of-payments cycle in terms of the elasticity approach, see Appendix to Chapter 5.
5 For an analysis of Japan's balance of payments following the same approach, see EPA (1985)
6 This section is based on Kwan (1990b).
7 This section is based on Kwan (1991c).
8 The Hong Kong dollar has been pegged to the US dollar since October 1983 when the Hong Kong dollar plummeted in the foreign exchange market amidst anxiety over the political future of Hong Kong. Despite such major shocks to the economy as Black Monday in October 1987 and the Tiananmen incident in June 1989, the Hong Kong dollar has remained stable against the US dollar in the foreign exchange market since the current system was introduced. The deviation of the market rate from the official rate of US$1=HK$7.8 has been minimal, and confidence in the Hong Kong dollar has been firmly established. The authorities have openly stated that the major objective of exchange-rate policy is to maintain the official parity rate and are determined in achieving this at all cost. Indeed,

in December 1987, when the Hong Kong dollar was under appreciation pressure, the Hong Kong Association of Banks changed its rules to enable banks to charge negative interest rates on short-term deposits over HK$1 million effective 10 March 1988.

9   This section is based on Kwan (1991d).
10 For the flying-geese model, see Chapter 5.
11 There is a large gap between US and Chinese statistics on bilateral trade. For example, while US statistics show a bilateral deficit of $10.4 billion with China in 1990, China claims to run a deficit of $1.4 billion against the United States. The difference between the two sets of figures seems to be too large to be explained away by the asymmetry in how the CIF (cost, insurance and freight) factor is treated in import and export statistics (which is usually cited as a major reason accounting for disparities in bilateral trade balances reported by the two countries involved). The gap between US and Chinese statistics can be bridged by referring to indirect trade between China and the United States through Hong Kong. According to trade statistics published by the Hong Kong government, re-exports of Chinese goods to the United States multiplied nearly 10 times between 1984 and 1990 to reach $10.5 billion, while growth in re-exports of US goods to China was less remarkable. As a result, the balance of indirect trade between China and the United States through Hong Kong grew, in favour of China, from $0.7 billion in 1984 to $9.1 billion in 1990. When the bilateral trade gap between China and the United States is calculated by combining Chinese and Hong Kong statistics (which show direct and indirect trade respectively), it moves parallel to the bilateral trade gap claimed by the US side. The gap calculated in this way amounted to $7.7 billion in 1990, and the disparity between the Chinese and US figures is greatly reduced. The remaining discrepancy can be attributed to, in addition to the CIF factor just mentioned, the exclusion of indirect exports to China through Hong Kong in US statistics.
12 The approach here follows EPA (1990). For an analysis taking into account the asymmetry between the investing country and the export market, see the section on the Pacific trade triangle in Chapter 6.

3 EXCHANGE-RATE REALIGNMENT AND SHORT-TERM ECONOMIC FLUCTUATIONS

1   This chapter is based on Kwan (1991c).
2   The small-country assumption allows us to focus on the supply side because aggregate demand is taken to be infinitely elastic to price changes. It also implies that fluctuations in the local currency against the yen and/or dollar would not affect GNP through an alteration in the terms of trade. However, fluctuations in the local currency can affect GNP through a change in the real wage rate when rigidity in the short run is taken into consideration, as we shall see in Chapter 4. See Kyle (1976) and Sachs (1980).
3   The formulation of the model follows Findlay and Rodriguez (1977).

4 AN OPTIMAL PEG FOR THE ASIAN CURRENCIES

1 This chapter is based on Kwan (1992)

2 Under the current system, certificates of indebtedness (CIs), which the two note-issuing banks (the Hongkong and Shanghai Bank and the Chartered Bank) are required to hold as cover for the issue of Hong Kong dollar notes, are issued and redeemed by the Exchange Fund at a fixed exchange rate of HK$7.8 = US$1. The two note-issuing banks in turn extend this rate to their note transactions with all other banks in Hong Kong. In the foreign exchange market, the exchange rate of the Hong Kong dollar continues to be determined by forces of supply and demand. However, the interplay of arbitration and competition between banks ensures that the market exchange rate stays close to the official rate (GIS, 1991). The government announced in January 1993 that the Bank of China would be granted the right to issue Hong Kong dollar notes, effective May 1994. This would expand the number of note-issuing banks to three, with other features of the system remaining basically unchanged.

3 The only exception is the Singapore dollar, whose exchange rate against the dollar has followed very closely the yen–dollar rate since mid-1990. Regressing the former on the latter for the period from April 1990 to December 1992 shows that the elasticity is as high as 0.635. That is, a 1.0 per cent appreciation of the yen against the dollar tends to drive up the Singapore dollar against the dollar by 0.635 per cent. This period, however, lies entirely outside the sample period used in Frankel's estimation.

4 For a survey of the literature on optimal pegs, see Williamson (1982). At a more general level, there is also a substantial literature that considers the optimal exchange regimes for developing countries, which usually focuses on the advantages and disadvantages of fixed versus flexible exchange rates (see Aghevli, Khan and Montiel, 1991 and Balassa, 1990). There seems to be general agreement that freely-floating exchanges rates are either not feasible or undesirable for most developing countries, which are characterized by limited capital markets, restrictions on capital flows and a prevalence of real shocks that need to be financed from reserves (see Black, 1976 and Wickham, 1985).

5 In a world where the major currencies are floating against one another, pegging to some currency, or basket of currencies, involves accepting fluctuations against all other currencies except those pegged to the same unit.

6 For a derivation of this result, see Bruno and Sachs (1985).

7 Abe (1990) analyses empirically the implications of alternative exchange-rate regimes on output, inflation and trade balances for Taiwan and South Korea using a Keynesian model for a small open economy. Argy, McKibbin and Siegloff (1989) examine the same issue in a three-country (Australia, the United States and Japan) model. In both cases the focus is on the macroeconomic variables themselves rather than on their volatility.

8 For a random variable X and a constant k, $\mathrm{Var}(kX) = k^2\mathrm{Var}(X)$

5 THE FLYING-GEESE PATTERN OF CHANGING TRADE STRUCTURE

1 This chapter is based on Kwan (1991a)

2 The flying-geese model is also known as the flying-wild-geese model or catching-up product cycle model.

3 Consumption (or domestic demand) is given by production plus imports minus exports. See Yamazawa (1990a).

4 The revealed comparative advantage (RCA) index provides an alternative measurement of international competitiveness. For a particular commodity (or group of commodities), the RCA index is calculated as its share of total exports of the country under consideration divided by its share of world exports (Balassa, 1965). For an analysis of the evolution of comparative advantage in the Asian NIEs using the RCA index, see, Amano (1991).

5 Primary commodities include SITC Sections 0 through 4 and Division 68. Machinery refers to SITC Section 7. Other manufactures represent SITC Sections 5, 6, 8 and 9 minus Division 68.

6 The US GNP deflator is used to derive per capita GNP at constant 1990 prices.

6 DEEPENING INTRA-REGIONAL INTERDEPENDENCE

1 This section is based on Kwan (1991a).

2 The complementarity index also depends on the classification of commodities used. Complementarity indexes among the Pacific countries for 1964–6 and 1979–81 based on SITC classification at the 3-digit level can be found in Drysdale (1988).

3 For an empirical study of the determinants of the export dependence ratio using cross-sectional data, see Yamazawa (1971).

4 See, for example, JETRO (1992), Takenaka (1992), Prestowitz (1988) and Bergsten and Cline (1985).

5 This section is based on Kwan (1991e).

6 Starting from a share of 20 per cent, for example, a 1.0 per cent appreciation of the yen raises the share by 0.058 (20%×0.29%) percentage point to 20.058 per cent.

7 EXPANSION OF NEW FRONTIERS

1 This chapter is based on Kwan (1991b).

2 The on-going acceleration of reform and open-door policy is a logical result of the harsh domestic and external conditions confronting China from 1989 through 1991. On the external front, while facing strict sanctions by many industrial countries in the wake of the Tiananmen incident in 1989, leaders in China witnessed the disintegration of the Soviet Bloc and the renunciation of socialism by the countries of Eastern Europe, as well as the Gulf War. On the domestic front, the repercussion of the Tiananmen incident and a stalemate in reforms caused various structural problems to come to the fore. The changes in the external environment also brought home to China the importance of science and

technology, the risk of assuming leadership of the socialist world, and the fatal consequences of the deteriorating performance of state-owned enterprises.

3   A more direct form of peace dividend in Asia is the conversion of military facilities to civil use. A typical example is the plan to transform the US Subic Naval Base in the Philippines to a commercial and industrial area after the retreat of the US forces in late 1992. Subic contains modern infrastructure that the rest of the Philippines lacks – a well-developed insulated deep harbour, ship repair facilities, airport, housing, telecommunications and recreation facilities. Although the US government has transferred most of its equipment out of Subic, the strategic location of the base makes it a prime site.

4   For simplicity, the following analysis will focus on the final equilibrium where marginal products of capital of the two countries have been equalized, but the conclusions concerning income and output remain basically the same when we focus on any point between the initial equilibrium and the final equilibrium instead.

5   For the complementary relations between Hong Kong and China, see Sung (1991).

6   The gap between GNP and GDP growth rate can be calculated roughly as follows. Assume that Hong Hong companies employ 3 million workers in China at a wage rate of $1200 a year. The total wage bill paid is then calculated at $3.6 billion. Further assume that each worker in Hong Kong earns $9,000 a year and productivity is twice as high as that in China. The labour cost required to produce the same level of output in Hong Kong is estimated at $13.5 billion. Profits for Hong Kong companies, given by the difference between the above two estimates, is around $10 billion. This is equivalent to about 10 per cent of Hong Kong GDP which amounted to $95.9 billion in 1992. The growth rate of GNP can be calculated as the weighted average of GDP growth and growth in profits earned abroad. With GDP growing 5.0 per cent and profits earned abroad growing 25 per cent, GNP growth is estimated at 7.0 per cent ($5.0\% \times 0.9 + 25\% \times 0.1$).

7   In a free trade area, member countries remove intra-area obstacles to free trade but retain their national tariffs against the rest of the world. Examples include the European Free Trade Area (EFTA) formed in 1960 and the US-Canada Free Trade Area formed in 1989. The customs union removes obstacles to free trade among members, as does the free trade area, but in addition the external tariffs are brought to the same level. A typical example is the EC before the end of 1992. In a common market, countries agree to the same policies as under the customs union, but in addition they remove obstacles to the free movement of labour and capital among member countries. The EC reached this stage in 1993. In an economic union, countries surrender national sovereignty over their exchange-rate, monetary and fiscal policies, as the the EC aims to achieve under the EMU (Economic and Monetary Union).

8   For an analysis of the Growth Triangle, see Ng and Wong (1991) and Lee (1991).

9   For a theoretical analysis of the Dutch disease, see Corden and Neary (1982).

8 THE ASIAN ECONOMIES IN THE 1990s

1 This chapter is based on Kwan (1993)

9 FORMATION OF A YEN BLOC

1 This chapter is based on Kwan (1992).
2 Outside academic circles, the broader definition is more commonly used. Typical examples are Maidment (1989) and Powell (1991).
3 For further details, see Tavlas and Ozeki (1991) and MOF (1992). The former also provides data for the use of the yen as a regional currency.
4 Figures are from Tavlas and Ozeki (1991).
5 The literature on the theory of optimum currency areas, starting from Mundell (1961), is surveyed by Ishiyama (1975) and Tower and Willett (1976). For a non-technical introduction of the subject, see De Grauwe (1992).
6 For an application of the theory of optimum currency areas to monetary integration in Europe, see Eichengreen (1991).
7 This is analogous to the two-stage 'world money game', with the first stage being the game of agreeing on choosing an international monetary regime and the second stage being the game of monetary interplays under given sets of rules (Hamada, 1985).
8 Flanders and Helpman (1979) reach a similar conclusion when considering the policy objective of stabilizing real income (real output adjusted for changes in the terms of trade) in a model that emphasizes the demand side of the economy.
9 When calculating the effective exchange rates for the Asian NIEs based on competitor weights, Balassa and Williamson (1987) assign weights for the yen ranging from 39.7 per cent (in the case of Hong Kong) to 66.9 per cent (in the case of Singapore). The United States is not even included in the list of competitors.
10 The view is shared by Emmott (1989), who also suggests that 'the sort of bloc to watch in Asia is quite likely to begin with currency arrangements rather than with any formal dismantling of trade barriers or development of regional institutions.'

BIBLIOGRAPHY

Abe, S. (1990) 'Exchange Rate Realignment Effects on Growth, Trade Balances, and Prices: Asian NIEs and ASEAN', in *Macroeconomic Structural Issues in the Asia-Pacific Economies*. The Japan National Committee for Pacific Economic Cooperation (March): Osaka.

Aghevli, B.B., Khan, M.S. and Montiel, P.J. (1991) 'Exchange Rate Policy in Developing Countries: Some Analytical Issues', *Occasional Papers* No. 78. International Monetary Fund (March).

Akamatsu, K. (1962) 'A Historical Pattern of Economic Growth in Developing Countries', *The Developing Economies* (March–August).

Amano, A. (1991) 'Evolution of Comparative Advantage in Manufacturing in the Asian NIEs', Working Paper 9112, School of Business Administration, Kobe University: Kobe, Japan.

Argy, V., McKibbin W. and Siegloff, E. (1989) 'Exchange-rate Regimes for a Small Economy in a Multi-Country World', *Princeton Studies in International Finance* No. 67, Princeton University: Princeton, New Jersey.

Bacha, E.L. (1981) 'The Impact of the Float on LDCs: Latin American Experience in the 1970s', in Williamson, J. (ed.) *Exchange Rate Rules*, Macmillan: London.

Balassa, B. (1961) *The Theory of Economic Integration*, Richard. D. Irwin: Homewood, Ill.

—— (1965) 'Trade Liberalization and "Revealed" Comparative Advantage', *The Manchester School* (Vol. 43, No. 2).

—— (1990) 'Exchange Rate Regimes for LDCs', in E. Claassen (ed.) *International and European Monetary Systems*, Heinemann Professional Publishing: Oxford.

—— and Williamson, J. (1987) 'Adjusting to Success: Balance of Payments Policy in the East Asian NICs', *Policy Analyses in International Economics* 17, Institute for International Economics: Washington.

Bergsten, C.F. and Cline, W.R. (1985) 'The United States-Japan Economic Problem, *Policy Analyses in International Economics* 13, Institute for International Economics: Washington.

Black, S.W. (1976) 'Exchange Rate Policies for Less developed Countries in a World of Floating Rates', *Essays in International Finance* No. 119, Princeton University: Princeton, New Jersey.

Branson, W.H. and Katseli-Papaefstratiou, L.T. (1980) 'Income Instability, Terms of Trade, and the Choice of an Exchange Rate Regime', *Journal of Development Economics* (March).

Bruno, M. and Sachs, J.D. (1985) *Economics of Worldwide Stagflation* (Chapter 3), Harvard University Press: Cambridge, Massachusetts.

Chen, E.K.Y. (1990) 'An Economic Outlook for Asia-Pacific in a Rapidly Changing International Environment, with Special Reference to Hong Kong', in *Asia Club Papers*, No. 1, Tokyo Club Foundation for Global Studies: Tokyo (June).

Connolly, M. (1982) 'The Choice of an Optimum Currency Peg for a Small Open Country', *Journal of International Money and Finance* (August).

Corden, W.M. and Neary, J.P. (1982) 'Booming Sector and De-industrialization in a Small Open Economy', *The Economic Journal* (Vol. 92, December).

Crokett, A.D. and Nsouli, S.M. (1977) 'Exchange Rate Policies for Developing Countries', *Journal of Development Studies* (January).

De Grauwe, P. (1992) *The Economics of Monetary Integration*, Oxford University Press.

Drysdale, P. (1988) *International Economic Pluralism – Economic Policy in East Asia and the Pacific*, Columbia University Press.

Eichengreen, B. (1991) 'Is Europe an Optimum Currency Area?' *NBER Working Papers*. No. 3579, National Bureau of Economic Research (January).

Emmott, B. (1989) *The Sun Also Sets*, Simon and Schuster: London.

EPA (1985) *Economic Survey of Japan*, Economic Planning Agency: Tokyo.

—— (1990) *Nihon to Sekai wo Kaeru Kaigai-Chokusetsu-Toshi (Foreign Direct Investment That Changes Japan and the World)*, In Japanese, Economic Planning Agency: Tokyo.

Findlay, R. and Rodriguez, C.A. (1977) 'Intermediate Imports and Macroeconomic Policy under Flexible Exchange Rates', *Canadian Journal of Economics*, Vol. 10.

Flanders, M.J. and Helpman, E. (1979). 'An Optimal Exchange Rate Peg in a World of General Floating', *Review of Economic Studies* (July).

Frankel, J.A. (1991a) 'Is a Yen Bloc Forming in Pacific Asia?' in R. O'Brien (ed.) *Finance and the International Economy: 5, The AMEX Bank Review Prize Essays*, Oxford University Press.

—— (1991b) 'On the Dollar and the Yen', *Pacific Basin Working Paper Series* No. PB91-04, Center for Pacific Basin Monetary and Economic Studies, Federal Reserve Bank of San Francisco (May).

Friedman, B.M. (1988) *Day of Reckoning*, Random House: New York.

GIS (1991) *Hong Kong 1991 – A Review of 1990*, Hong Kong Government Information Services: Hong Kong.

Grubel, H.J. and Lloyd, P.J. (1975) *Intra-industry Trade: The Theory and Measurement of International Trade in Differentiated Products*, Wiley: New York.

Hamada, K. (1985) *The Political Economy of International Monetary Interdependence*, MIT Press: Cambridge, Massachusetts.

Holloway, N. (1990) 'Building a Yen Bloc', *Far Eastern Economic Review* (11 October).

IMF (1992) *Exchange Arrangements and Exchange Restrictions* (Annual Report), International Monetary Fund.

Ishiyama, Y. (1975) 'The Theory of Optimum Currency Areas: A Survey', *IMF Staff Papers*, International Monetary Fund (July).

JETRO (1992) *White Paper on International Trade of Japan*, Japan External Trade Organization: Tokyo.

Johnson, H.G. (1958) *International Trade and Economic Growth*, Allen & Unwin: London.

Kindleberger, C.P. (1968), *International Economics*. 4th ed., Irwin: Homewood, Ill.

Kwan, C.H. (1990a) 'Mega-trends in the Asian Economies,' in *Asia Club Papers*, No. 1, Tokyo Club Foundation for Global Studies: Tokyo (June).

—— (1990b) 'New Era in Eastern Europe: Implications for Asia', in *Nomura Investment Review*, Nomura Research Institute: Tokyo (August).

—— (1991a) 'The Emerging Pattern of Trade and Interdependence in the Pacific Region', in *Tokyo Club Papers* (No. 4, Part 2), Tokyo Club Foundation for Global Studies: Tokyo.

—— (1991b) 'New Frontiers of the Asian Economies', in *Nomura Investment Review*, Nomura Research Institute: Tokyo (March).

—— (1991c) 'The Impact of Exchange-Rate Realignment on the Asian Economies – An Expanded Analysis', in *Asia Club Papers* (No. 2), Tokyo Club Foundation for Global Studies: Tokyo (May).

—— (1991d) 'The Flying-Geese Pattern of Pacific Trade Imbalances', *Nomura Investment Review*, Nomura Research Institute: Tokyo (July).

—— (1991e) 'The Asian NIEs as a Built-in Stabilizer for Japanese Exports', *Nomura Investment Review*, Nomura Research Institute: Tokyo (September).

—— (1992) 'An Optimal Peg for the Asian Currencies and the Implications for a Yen Bloc', in *Asia Club Papers* (No. 3), Tokyo Club Foundation for Global Studies: Tokyo (April).

—— (1993) 'The Asian Economies in the 1990s', in *Nomura Asia Focus*, Nomura Research Institute (February).

Kyle, J.F. (1976) *The Balance of Payments in a Monetary Economy*. Princeton University Press: Princeton.

Lee, T.Y, (1991) *Growth Triangle*, Institute of Southeast Asian Studies: Singapore.

Linder, B. (1961) *An Essay on Trade and Transformation*, John Wiley: New York.

Lipschitz, L. (1979) 'Exchange Rate Polices for a Small Developing Country, and the Selection of an Appropriate Standard', *IMF Staff Papers*, International Monetary Fund (September).

—— and Sundararajan, V. (1980) 'An Optimal Exchange Rate Peg in a World of Generalized Floating', *IMF Staff Papers*, International Monetary Fund (March).

MacDougall, G.A.D. (1958) 'The Benefits and Costs of Private Investment from Abroad: A Theoretical Approach', *Economic Record*, Vol. 36.

Maidment, P. (1989) 'The Yen Block – A New Balance in Asia', *The Economist* (July 15).

MOF (1992) *Annual Report of the International Finance Bureau*, Japanese Ministry of Finance (in Japanese).

Mundell, R. (1961) 'A Theory of Optimum Currency Areas', *American Economic Review* (September).

Ng, C.Y. and Wong, P.K. (1991) 'The Growth Triangle – A Market Driven Response?' in *Asia Club Papers*, No. 2, Tokyo Club Foundation for Global Studies: Tokyo.

NRI (1991) 'Medium-Term Economic Outlook for Japan and the World', *Nomura Economic Report*, No. 12, Nomura Research Institute (March).

Park, Y.C. and Park, W.A. (1990) 'Exchange Rate Policy for the East Asian NICs', *KDI Working Paper* No. 9010, Korea Development Institute (May).

Powell, B. (1991) 'The Yen Bloc – Sayonara, America', *Newsweek* (5 August).

Prestowitz, C.V. Jr, (1988) *Trading Places*, Basic Books: New York.

Sachs, J. (1980) 'Wages, Flexible Exchange Rates, and Macroeconomic Policy', *Quarterly Journal of Economics* (June).

Sung, Y.W. (1991) *The China-Hong Kong Connection*, Cambridge University Press: Cambridge.

Suzuki, Y. (1989) *Japan's Economic Performance and International Role* (Chapter 4), Tokyo University Press: Tokyo.

Takenaka, H. (1992) 'U.S.-Japan Policy Coordination in the Asia-Pacific Context', in Okuizumi, K., Calder, K. E. and Gong, G.W. (Eds), *The U.S.-Japan Relationship in East and Southeast Asia*, Center for Strategic and International Studies: Washington.

Tavlas, G.S. and Ozeki, Y. (1991) 'The Japanese Yen as an International Currency', *IMF Working Paper*, International Monetary Fund (January).

Tower, E. and Willett, T.D. (1976) 'The Theory of Optimum Currency Areas and Exchange Rate Flexibility', *Princeton Special Papers in International Finance* No. 11.

Vernon, R. (1966) 'International Investment and International Trade in the Product Cycle', *Quarterly Journal of Economics* (May).

Wickham. P. (1985) 'The Choice of Exchange Rate Regime in Developing Countries', *IMF Staff Papers*, International Monetary Fund (June).

Williamson, J. (1982) 'A Survey of the Literature on the Optimal Peg', *Journal of Development Economics* (Vol. 11).

World Bank (1985) *World Development Report* (Chapter 4), Oxford University Press.

Yamazawa, I. (1971) 'Structural Change in World Trade Flows', *Hitotsubashi Journal of Economics* (February).

―― (1990a) *Economic Development and International Trade: The Japanese Model*, East-West Center, Resource Systems Institute: Honolulu, Hawaii.

―― (1990b) 'Gearing the Japanese Economy to International Harmony', *The Developing Economies*, (March).

INDEX

Abe, S. 173
AFTA (ASEAN Free Trade Area)
133, 134
Aghevli, B.B. 173
Akamatsu, K. 10, 81
Amano, A. 174
ANZCERTA 133
APEC (Asia-Pacific Economic
Cooperation) 133, 135
appreciation of currencies (mainly
yen) 27–9, 32, 89; and exchange
rate realignment 41, 43–7, 49, 55;
and optimal currency peg
65, 68
Argy, V. 173
ASEAN countries (Indonesia,
Malaysia, Philippines, Singapore,
Thailand) 1–3, 5–6, 9, 12–13;
balance of payments 18, 22–3,
25–6, 29–35, 38–40; economies
in 1990s 143, 144, 145–8, 149,
150, 152–4; exchange rate
realignment 13, 15, 41–7, 48–54,
56–9; expansion of new frontiers
119–20, 123, 127, 132–5, 175;
flying-geese pattern 11, 82, 83,
85, 87–97, 99; intra-regional
interdependence 101–5, 112–13;
optimal currency peg 65, 67, 70,
73, 75; yen bloc, formation of
7–8, 157, 162, 166–7, 169
ASEAN Free Trade Area (AFTA)
133, 134
Asia-Pacific Economic Cooperation
133, 135
Asia-Pacific, economic

interdependence in see ASEAN;
Asian NIEs; China; economies in
1990s; exchange rate; expansion
of new frontiers; flying-geese;
Indochina; intra-regional
interdependence; Japan; optimal
currency peg
'Asian Currency Unit' (ACU) 167
Asian NIEs (Hong Kong, Singapore,
South Korea, Taiwan) 1–3, 4, 6,
9, 12–13; balance of payments
18, 21–9, 31–5, 38–40, 171–2;
economies in 1990s 142, 143,
145, 147–8, 149, 150–1;
exchange rate realignment 13, 14,
15, 41–8, 49–57, 59; expansion
of new frontiers 119, 120, 123–4,
127–30, 131–2, 134, 136–9,
175; flying-geese pattern 11, 82,
83–97, 99, 174; intra-regional
interdependence 100–18; optimal
currency peg 63–4, 65–6, 68–9,
73, 75, 173; yen bloc, formation
of 6–7, 8, 157, 159–60, 166–7,
169, 176; see also South China
Economic Zone
asset liquidator stage 19, 20
Association of Southeast Asian
Nations see ASEAN
Australia 86, 87–9, 135
automobile industry 82–3

Bacha, E.L. 71
balance of payments and exchange
rate realignment 15, 18–40,
171–2; and foreign direct

181